TABLE OF CONTENT

PREFACE

The idea to write this book came from my love for information risk management, the desire to formulate a framework that will allow me to rapidly but effectively bring together the information needed and present it in a way that would be defensible and useable. The main driving force was to give information security risk professionals more needed practical approaches and case studies, and best-practice guides and examples that can assist them in their enterprise security risk management programs. As security consultants, we are committed to helping our customers find solutions to their security problems. This book is structured to focus on the practical implementation of risk assessment. The book is structured to go straight to the actions that a risk assessor will take to assess risk and provide recommendations that meet the business needs and risk appetite. The book is focused on specific implementation guidance rather than aspirational messages and vague high-level suggestions.

Enterprise Information Security Risk Assessment details a methodology that adopts the best part of some established frameworks and teaches the reader how to use the available information to conduct a risk assessment that will identify high-risk assets. The book will provide you with the tools needed to execute a practical security risk assessment and adopt a suitable process for you.

Celestin Ntemngwa, PhD, MBA, CISA, CISM

Celestin spent much time in IT security, infrastructure, incident response, and risk management for on-prem and cloud environments. Well-versed in direct and remote systems analysis and investigation with strong critical thinking, communication, and a sense of ownership. His career as a security consultant is built on my diverse background, from teaching sciences and mathematics in secondary high school and university to owning and managing a business in information security and risk management. This background has enriched him with many equalities that he applies in career. Celestin has been a science teacher and professor, where he had to learn to know his students' diverse learning styles and needs and use multiple teaching approaches to meet those learning needs. He spent much time planning lessons and crafting the lesson objectives to empower the students to be scientifically literate. In addition to that, he had to collaborate with colleagues, do research, and present findings at national and international meetings. As a business owner, he plans the business phases, processes, from operations to financial management and recruit the right people to collaborate and meet objectives.

He is security consultant and risk advisor with one of the big four consulting firms where he helps companies stay on track and deal with risks that could unhinge their business survival.

His background has helped him tremendously as an information security professional. When planning this book, he had to spend much time crafting the various sections and chapters' objectives in the book. That was the hard part of the work! Fortunately, opportunities as a consultant had allowed a breadth of experience partnering with organizations across many industries.

Thus, Celestin has a combination of business, technical, and people skills through his experience in business management, education, security management, including risk management, security awareness training and readiness, and security standards compliance. This has been a tremendous asset in his career and in writing this book.

For years as a consultant, he has helped clients design, build, assess, and improve their risk management programs. He has led and executed cybersecurity and maturity assessments against industry frameworks (ISO 27001/27002, NIST 800 series, GDPR, and HIPAA / HITECH). Worked on and managed a diverse range of Cybersecurity, Technology Risk, and Privacy client engagements. He has helped develop Cloud solutions that meet regulatory requirements, including but not limited to EU GDPR, PCI, SOX, HIPAA, etc.

Celestin's approach to building adequate security is to follow and safeguard the organization's systems and data, identifying the risks and ensuring robust controls are in place. He understands business needs, the daily trade-off between the organization's risk appetite and business delivery. As a result, he delivers pragmatic advice. Dealing with stakeholders, setting expectations, and communicating in a language that people understand is essential to winning over awareness, comprehension, and collaboration.

He has assisted clients in incident response and remediation efforts by providing strategic short, medium, and long-term remediation recommendations to directors and C-level executives while also providing tactical recommendations to specialists to improve an organization's security posture.

He has helped clients expand their Cybersecurity and Risk Advisory practice and identified potential cybersecurity risks in customer environments. Proposed tailored solutions to address customer security threats and risks. Assisted with managing all aspects of sales from start to finish. Helped businesses meet strategic and operational goals by identifying opportunities to deploy new technologies and create a streamlined process. Assessed results and ensured a high level of customer satisfaction. He also has a background in working in security operations centers. I have

He has independently performed 100+ security reviews, audits, core technology controls, risk assessment engagements, segregation of duties, and logical access for a range of clients in diverse industries. He has evaluated and documented customer technical needs relating to IT security.

Celestin has developed and continue learning about AI/Machine Learning, emerging technologies, and intelligent ecosystems. He has built machine learning models to solve business problems and document data extraction. He has and continues to develop extensive knowledge of machine learning algorithms, techniques, available implementations in python (e.g., NumPy, SciPy, Pandas) and frameworks (e.g., TensorFlow).

To learn more about Dr. Ntemngwa and how to work with him, visit

https://drcelestinntemngwa.com/

ACKNOWLEDGEMENTS

Many people are responsible for supporting, encouraging, and allowing me to work in this field that I love so dearly. A big thank you to all of them.

I want to thank my wife and my kids, Awungjia, Ivy, and Jordan Ntemngwa, for their support when working on this book. They have always been there for me.

INTRODUCTION

Defining an enterprise

Information technology is everywhere in the business world, and its decisions affect the entire organization. Information technology resources support different business functions and processes. Thus, any changes in the IT resource could have profound repercussions or effects on the enterprise.

What is an enterprise? Enterprise is a fluid term, which comprises all technologies and all technology-related policies associated with the services that an organization provides to its customers, associates, users, etc.

An enterprise requires planning to control its growth into valuable areas, guidance to maintain its security and integrity during operation, and governance to manage the strategic objectives. There is a need for a stable but agile enterprise that can respond to the business's changing needs (integrating new technologies) while maintaining its stability and continuity of operations.

It is also essential that the technology selected in an enterprise meets the business objectives, security requirements, performs efficiently, supports the business processes, and is cost-effective. Technology should support business processes and align with the organization's strategic goals.

The value of information to the enterprise

All organizations collect, process, store, and transmit information in different forms. The information, together with the various processes of networks, systems, and people involved in the processing and protection, are critical assets to the organization. An asset is defined in general terms as something valuable or useful. IT assets could be software or hardware. These assets are beneficial to the organization and must be well protected from any risks. Adversarial and non-adversarial are continually attacking the assets while related systems, processes, and personnel have inherent vulnerabilities. When threat sources act on vulnerabilities, it results in security risks to the organization. Within the organization, business processes and systems are continuously changing, and these changes can generate vulnerabilities that can lead to risks. One of the main ways to reduce security risks is through adequate information security. Adequate information and cybersecurity are attained by employing suitable sets of countermeasures or controls. These controls ensure the organization's business and security goals are achieved.

Enterprise information security

An organization's information needs to be secured. The organization's current security practices and processes should be concentrated on managing and mitigating risks associated with the confidentiality, integrity, and availability of the organization's information. Information security is essential, mostly as the information or data is related to IT resources and systems' operation and maintenance. Various business units within the organization have to be concerned about security issues such as data compromise, the inadvertent disclosure or release of sensitive or protected data, theft of equipment containing the organization's data. A successful enterprise architecture initiative begins with creating a straightforward well-developed security program with precise and identified requirements and achievable goals.

To effectively manage a security program in the EA, we break it down into smaller, manageable projects. Breaking it down has benefits including, but not limited to ensuring that any new technology meets our organization's needs before full implementation, establishing clear distinctive goals that technology implementers can easily understand. Smaller, manageable projects lessen user's resistance to change by taking things one step at a time.

Security in enterprise architecture is more than merely the sum of its parts. Security professionals must be implemented in a planned manner; they should not add elements ad hoc. The organization should consider conforming to an information security standard to increase its enterprise security program's effectiveness and demonstrate that the organization follows information security best practices. The difference between project and program has to be clearly articulated and understood. Projects have a beginning and an end while programs are continuous. For example, a risk assessment is a project, while risk management is a program. Senior management has to understand that installing an intrusion detection system (IDS) is a project that does not mean the system will always be secured. But, that there is a need for ongoing maintenance, monitoring, and updates. Thus, IDS installation is a project, but security, in general, is a program, which is continuous.

The goals of information security

Information security professionals have extensive and critical tasks to safeguard the organization's valuable assets, such as information and systems. When we think of information security objectives, we usually use a model known as the CIA triad. CIA stands for confidentiality, integrity, and availability. This model emphasizes the three most crucial functions of information security professionals in an enterprise: confidentiality, integrity, and availability.

Confidentiality ensures that only authorized persons have access to the organization's information and resource. Confidentiality consumes most security professionals' time. Adversaries seeking to undercut confidentiality usually engage in disclosure attacks, making sensitive information available to the general public or specific individuals without the information owner's consent.

Information Security professionals are also responsible for protecting the integrity of an organization's information. This means that they have to ensure that there are no unauthorized changes to information or data. These unauthorized changes can be in the form of an adversary or hacker seeking to intentionally modify the information or disrupt a service that inadvertently affects data stored in a system. In either case, it is the information security professional's responsibility to prevent these gaps in integrity.

Another goal of information security is availability; ensure that authorized or legitimate persons can gain access to information when they need it. If users fail to access essential company records or systems, that absence of availability could profoundly impact the business. Adversary seeking to undermine availability conducts attacks known as denial of service attacks. These attacks aim to either overpower a system or cause it to crash, denying legitimate users the access they need.

Organization information security requirements

For adequate security controls to be successfully established, implemented, monitored, reviewed, and improved, the organization has to start by identifying its security requirements. Figure1 shows an overview of organization information security requirements.

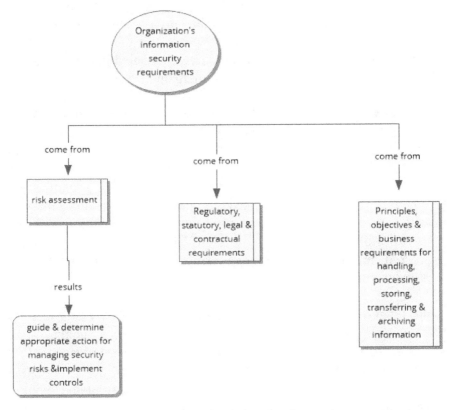

Figure1: Organization information security requirements overview

WHAT IS RISK?

When it comes to the definition of risk, context is essential. The risk could have a different meaning in a different context. For instance, there is a financial risk, economic risk, security risk, transportation risk, etc. The definition of risk holds much ambiguity. This ambiguity in risk definition could hinder its proper understanding. Context thus plays a crucial role in the description of risk. This implies that it is probably difficult to have a universally accepted definition of risk.

Moreover, risk assessment varies depending on the business department in an organization and the business or process objectives. Risk assessment can be conducted at the departmental level in an organization or organization-wide. However, all the risk assessments performed at various departments could be channeled into a centralized risk assessment unit for reporting and amalgamation.

Risk is an ever-present part of the business world. Organizations set strategic and business objectives with the understanding that those objectives will be under the constant threat of risks. The organization has to manage risks that threaten the attainment of those objectives. Risks manifest themselves in different ways. An organization's information is valuable and needs proper protection. For adequate security to be put in place, one needs to understand the threats and risks to the information or any organization's asset. When information is considered an asset to the organization, an information security assessment must be conducted to understand the potential dangers that the asset is exposed to. Risk can be defined as a potential or real event(s) that diminishes the likelihood of achieving business objectives. Risk creates uncertainty about the organization's goals. It is characterized by reference to potential events and consequences. Risk is expressed as consequences of adverse events and the likelihood of the events occurring. If an attacker initiates a Distributed Denial of Services attack (DDOS attack) on the company's public website, that is a threat event. There is a likelihood that that attack might be successful. If there is a vulnerability in the server that hosts the website, the attacker could exploit that to increase the chance of the attack being successful. If it is successful, it creates an adverse impact (if users cannot access the website, the company loses money, loses customers, etc.). Therefore, the risk results from the attacker exploiting the vulnerability to produce a DDOS attack, which leads to a denial of legitimate users' access to the company's website, causing the company financial loss. In NIST SP 800-37, the risk is defined as " a measure of the extent to which a potential circumstance or event threatens an entity, and function of: the adverse impacts that would arise if the circumstance or event occurs, and the likelihood of occurrence."

Figure 2 below shows a summary of the risk.

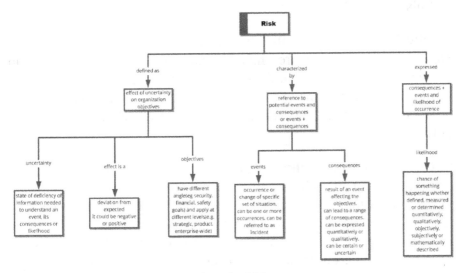

Figure2: Risk summary

Risk Assessment

In the world of information security, everywhere contains risks. Risks could come from hackers, malware, loss of devices, missing security patches, etc. There is much risk for information security professionals to address. Addressing each risk takes resources such as time, skilled personnel, and money. As a result, information security professionals, in collaboration with other organization senior management, must prioritize the risk lists to spend resources where they will have tremendous security benefits. That is where risk assessment comes into play.

Risk assessment is a process where facing an organization is identified and triaged based on the likelihood of their occurrence and the anticipated impact on the organization's functions or operations.

Risk assessment is one of the critical components of an organizational risk management process depicted in NIST Special Publication 800-39. Risk assessment focuses on identifying the security risks that the organization's network, applications, and software face. In risk assessment, the security risks are identified, analyzed, and classified as qualitative (low, medium, high, or critical) or quantitative. Once the risks have been identified, analyzed, and ranked, those conducting the assessment propose control or mitigation measures. The recommended controls are based on the priority of the risks.

In daily life, people often use the terms threat, risk, and vulnerability interchangeably. These are three distinct concepts. A threat is an external force that jeopardizes the security of an organization's information and systems. Threats may be naturally occurring, such as tornadoes and floods, or humanmade such as hacking and identity theft.

Threats exist independently and cannot be controlled. A threat vector is a method that an attacker uses to get to a target. This could be malware, physical intrusion, hacker toolkit, social engineering, or other hacking techniques. Vulnerabilities are weaknesses in the security controls that a threat might exploit to destabilize the confidentiality, integrity, or availability of the information or systems. Vulnerabilities include lack of security training, using legacy equipment with missing patches, flawed firewall rules, security misconfigurations, inadequate physical security, etc.

In terms of control, we do have control over vulnerabilities. We can search for vulnerabilities in our environment and remediate them before bad actors exploit them. Security professionals usually scan for vulnerabilities and remediate them. Risks occur when your environment contains both a vulnerability and a related threat that could exploit the vulnerability. If there is no threat, and there is no vulnerability, then there is no risk. Some main attributes considered in risk assessment includes **confidentiality, integrity, authentication, availability, resilience, and non-repudiation**.

Confidentiality

Testing confidentiality involves verifying whether the information, resources, and services, are accessible only to expected users and only when requested. The assessment consists of verifying if unauthorized users are allowed access to resources, verify if the information stored or transmitted is encrypted, and analyze the format in which data is displayed to the users when requested.

Confidentiality could be rated as Low, Moderate, or High.

Key questions to ask when assessing confidentiality of a system:

How sensitive is the data that is stored, transported, and processed by the system?

What will be the impact on the organization's business/mission if the data is compromised?

Integrity

Integrity is assessed by making sure that the information received is unaltered in transit. Also, the information the user received is updated and correct. When using the NIST framework for controls, integrity can be controlled using NIST 800-53 S1-7.

Integrity could be rated as Low, Moderate, or High.

How accurate is the organization's data, and how does it impact the business /mission if incorrectly modified?

Availability

Availability is tested to make sure the application is available as needed with minimal downtime. The tester also ensures a regular back up of data and information so that it is readily available when needed.

Availability= Low, Moderate or High

What is the impact on the organization's business/mission if the data is not available when needed?

Authentication

In authentication, the user is digitally identified before being granted access to the enterprise system. During the assessment, the system that gives this access is tested and validated for efficacy in granting access to only identified users who are who they say they are.

Why Risk Assessments in the Enterprise?

Information technology and information systems help organizations to execute their missions and business functions successfully. Information systems include different entities that range from specialized systems such as telecommunication systems to office networks. Information systems involve the management of the information, and it has not just the technology components involved but also the people and processes. It is essential to understand how to implement information systems to support companies and organizations internally.

Information systems are often the target of threats that can negatively affect the organizational assets and operations, personnel, other organizations (such as business partners), and even the nation. Threats to information systems can explore vulnerabilities (both known and unknown) to compromise the confidentiality, integrity, or availability of the information that the systems processes, stores, or transmits. There are numerous threats directed at information systems.

These threats pose a significant danger to organizations and should be proactively analyzed and mitigated. To successfully diagnose and minimize threats to the organizations, all the organization (leaders, managers) must understand their responsibilities in managing information security risk. The National Institute of Standards (NIST), in its Special Publication 30 Rev 1, highlighted the importance of managers and business leaders at all levels to understand their responsibilities and being held accountable for managing security risk.

The security risk is "the risk associated with the operation and use of information systems that support the missions and business functions of their organizations"(NIST SP 800-30).

Risk assessment is to:

- Analyze the effectiveness of the current security controls that protect the enterprise assets and determine the probability of losses to those assets.

- Help identify, classify, assess, and prioritize risk to business operations such as mission, processes, functions, reputation, assets, individuals, other organizations resulting from the operation and use of information systems.

- Find problems and security holes before attackers do.

- Measure the security posture of the organization.

- Understand the existing system and environment.

- Provide evidence that decision-makers can use to make risk-based decisions.

- Identify risks through the analysis of information or data gathered.

- Obtain a snapshot of the security risks that might compromise the CIA of the company's information asset.

- Help organizations select appropriate security controls based on an organization's needs and a cost-benefit analysis.

- Inform and support risk-based decision making and support risk responses.

A key benefit of risk assessment is its potential to help risk responses from decision-makers. Risk assessment supports the decision-making process by providing information about relevant threats to organizations, or those threats can come from other organizations. A risk assessment also identifies internal and external vulnerabilities to the organizations. The risk assessment also uses qualitative or quantitative methods to determine the impact or potential harm to the organization if a threat explores specific vulnerabilities. Furthermore, risk assessment computes the likelihood that the effect or damage will take place.

There are numerous ways to assess security risk. Depending on the method used, security risk could be done in different steps or phases. The steps or stages could have different names. The security risk assessment process is conducted as a project. It begins with a project definition, preparation, technical and administrative data gathering, risk analysis, risk mitigation, and controls recommendations. The risk assessment is described in more detail later in this book. The risk assessment process is part of enterprise risk management.

RISK ASSESSMENT TECHNIQUES

Quantitative risk assessment

Quantitative risk assessment techniques use objective numeric scores to assess likelihood and impact, mostly in terms of dollars. When we gather quantitative data about the organization's assets and risks, we could use it to produce data-informed decisions about risks. Quantitative risk assessment is the process of using numeric data to help in risk decisions. Quantitative risk assessment is done on a single risk/asset pairing. For example, security professionals might assess the risk of a tornado to a data center facility. As they conduct this assessment, they first determine the values for different variables. The first variable is the asset value (AV). AV is the estimated value in dollars of the asset. Security risk assessors can use different options to determine an asset's value. They can use the original cost method, which looks at invoices from an asset purchased and uses the acquisition or purchase prices to determine the asset value. While this method is the easiest, it is often criticized; the cost to replace an asset fluctuates since asset prices can change with time.

The next technique is the depreciated cost technique, which is an accounting favorite. It starts with the asset's original cost and then reduces the asset's value over time as it ages. The other technique is the depreciation technique, which uses an estimate of the asset's useful life and then steadily decreases the asset value until it reaches zero at the end of its projected lifetime. The replacement cost technique is the most popular because it produces results closest to the estimated actual costs that an organization will incur if a risk occurs. The replacement cost technique peruses current supplier prices to ascertain the actual cost of replacing an asset in the current market. Then it uses that cost as the asset's value. For example, if the data center is valued at $10 million, that is the actual amount needed to rebuild it if a tornado destroys the center.

The second variable to consider is the exposure factor(EF). The exposure factor estimates the percentage of the asset that will be destroyed if a risk occurs. For example, if we anticipate a tornado might ruin 50% of the data center, we will set the exposure factor for that tornado to 50%.

The next variable to consider in quantitative risk assessment is the single-loss expectancy or SLE. This SLE is the actual damage expected to happen if a risk occurs once. We can compute the SLE by multiplying the asset value(AV) by the exposure factor(EF). So, SLE = AV x EF

For example, if we value the data center at $10 million and expect that a tornado would cause 50% damage to the center, we compute the SLE as follows:

AV x EF = $10 million x 50% = $5 million

Thus, the tornado will cause $5 million in damage if it occurs once. The SLE gives us an idea of the impact of the risk.

Another variable that has to do with likelihood is the Annualized Rate of Occurrence (ARO).

The ARO is the number of times per year that we expect a risk to occur. For example, for the data center, if we determine that there is a 5% annual risk of a tornado in the area of the data center, it will mean that we can expect 0.05 tornados to occur each year in that area. The ARO is 0.05.

Finally, in risk analysis, we can combine the likelihood and impact values by computing the annualized loss expectancy, or ALE. ALE is the amount of money an organization would expect to lose each year from that risk. ALE represents a decent gauge of the overall risk to the organization. We compute the ALE as follows:

ALE = SLE x ARO

In the case of tornado risk to the data center, the SLE was 5 million, and the ARO was 0.05. Multiplying these together, we get an annualized loss expectancy of $250,000. This amount means that the organization would lose $250,000 each year from the risk of tornado damaging the data center. Note that this cost might not necessarily occur each year. Nevertheless, the damage that the organization incurs each time the tornado occurs and destroys the data center.

Qualitative Risk Assessment

Qualitative risk techniques utilize subjective judgments to assess risks. This subjective judgment usually involves categorizing risks as low, medium, or high on both the likelihood and impact scales. For example, a qualitative risk assessment chart is used. When analyzing a specific risk, we rate the likelihood as low, medium, or high and do the same for the impact. We then use the chart to categorize the overall risk. For instance, a high probability, high impact risk would be classified as a high risk, while a medium probability low impact risk would be categorized overall as low risk.

RISK MANAGEMENT

Risk management is the process of risk identification, evaluation assessment, and control. (ISO 3100 refers to it as the effect of uncertainty on objectives). Once the risks have been identified and evaluated, a series of coordinated applications or resources are implemented to minimize, monitor, and control the likelihood of the impact on the organization. Each organization has its overall business or organizational objectives. The risk could be considered an effect of uncertainty on the organizational goals. Organizations manage risk by identifying, analyzing, and evaluating if some controls or measures modify the risk. Organizations could use risk treatment to meet the risk criteria. Risk treatment here refers to a process undertaken by the organization to alter the risk. Risk criteria refer to some reference against which the organization evaluates the significance of the risk. Organizations communicate and consult stakeholders throughout the risk management process. Organizations also review and monitor the controls that modify the risk to ensure that no additional risk treatment is needed.

Organizations need to develop, implement, and frequently make improvements to a framework used to manage risk. The risk management framework consists of components that give the organizational structure and arrangements for designing, implementing, reviewing, monitoring, and improving risk management throughout the organization. Risk management integrates the risk management process in the organization strategy, governance, planning management, policies, values, and culture and reporting process. Risk management adopts a consistent approach with a comprehensive framework to effectively manage its risk across the organization. Risk management establishes context to underscore the organizational environment's objectives where it operates, its stakeholders, and its various risk criteria.

Risk management objectives

Risk management is aimed at better meeting the organization or business objectives. It enhances proactive management and governance to boost the confidence of stakeholders and the public. It helps with compliance with regulatory legal and business requirements. It improves the ability to identify threats, vulnerabilities, and opportunities. It enhances security controls to manage risk treatment resources and minimize losses efficiently.

If an organization already has a risk management process for particular risks, it can review its existing processes and practices using any appropriate standard. Risk management comprises an entire architecture (principles, framework, and processes) for managing risks.

Risk management Architecture

Risk management architecture is made up of three components. The three components are risk management principles, risk management framework, and risk management process. The components that guide the management of risk in an organization are based on value creation, which involves principles such as continual improvement, structured and comprehensive, inclusive, and dynamic. Managing risk is also based on leadership and its commitment that oversees the development of a framework for managing risk.

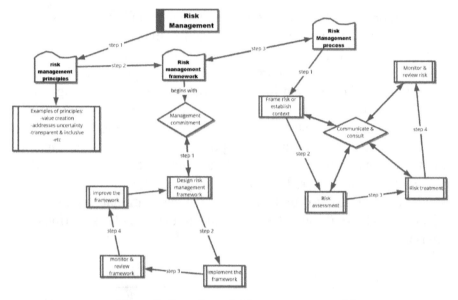

Figure 3: Overview of risk management architecture

Risk management principles and Guidelines

For an organization to succeed in its risk management endeavor, it must abide by certain principles. Some of the fundamental principles are described in the proceeding section. Figure 4 shows some risk management principles.

Figure 4: Risk management principles

Risk management should be inclusive and transparent to all business units and stakeholders. The stakeholders must be included in risk management at the right time. Mostly at the beginning of a risk management project. Stakeholders are organizations or people that can be affected by any decision made. Stakeholders and those who could influence the decisions, and those who believe that a decision or activity could affect them. The next risk management principle is to create value. Risk management contributes to the accomplishment of enterprise-wide business objectives. Risk management seeks to improve security regulatory compliance, project management, and change management processes. Risk management also enhances the decision-making process. It provides evidence-based information that supports the prioritization of actions and choices that decision-makers need to make. Risk management has a well-structured, reliable, repeatable method to produce consistent, reliable, and evidence-based resource data.

Another principle of risk management is that it uses the best information for its input. The risk management process uses inputs that are based on reliable sources. Some of the commonly used sources include stakeholder feedback, historical data, and expert judgment. However, this data might have some limitations that should be considered when using the result of the data processed. Risk management should address any uncertainties involved in risk. The uncertainties involved in risk management should be acknowledged in terms of the nature of the uncertainty and ways to address them.

Risk management should also respond to change. Changes occur regularly in most fast-paced organizations. For risk management to appropriately address risks, it has to react rapidly to changes within the organization. Risk management is sensitive to any change and makes the necessary adjustments or modifications whenever a change occurs. Change can happen because of the occurrence of an internal or external event. Other variables in the enterprise can change, such as new risk, acquisition of a new asset, etc. Risk management should be dynamic and responsive to change in the enterprise.

An organization should find and develop strategies to improve and support their risk management maturity continuously. Organizational objectives are critical to the best success of an organization. Achieving these objectives could be hindered by internal and external parties' intentions, capabilities, and perceptions. Risk management should seek to recognize these external and internal influences and take appropriate actions if necessary.

Risk management is part of the organization's processes. An organization should not treat risk management as a separate entity process from the rest of the organization processes. Instead, risk management should be considered an integral part of the entire enterprise processes and activities. Management understands that risk management is part of their responsibilities. Risk management has to be included in various enterprise strategic planning and change management activities and processes. Risk management should also be tailored to align with the organization's internal and external risk profile, a description of any set of risks, and its environment to achieve its objectives.

RISK MANAGEMENT FRAMEWORKS

Risk management frameworks provide proven, practical, time-tested techniques for conducting enterprise risk management. So, organizations do not have to design their risk management from scratch. One of the most commonly used risk management frameworks was created by the National Institute of Standards and Technology(NIST), a US federal government agency. Though the NIST risk management framework (RMF) process is mandatory for many government computer systems, it is not compulsory for private organizations. However, private organizations have widely adopted NIST RMF because of their helpful approach.

The framework can be found in NIST Special Publication 800-37and is available for free on NIST's website. For this book, we will do an overview of the six steps in the process.

NIST RMF has six steps involved in risk management, according to NIST.

Step 1: Categorize Information Systems.

Step 2: Select Security Controls.

Step 3: Implement Security Controls.

Step 4: Assess Security Controls.

Step 5: Authorize Information System.

Step 6: Monitor Security Controls.

Before starting the process, the organization should gather information from two categories: Technology architecture, including reference models, technical details, business process information, and information system boundaries. The second input to the process is organization-specific information, including the laws, regulations, and organization policies, the strategy of the organization, its priorities, resource availability, and supply chain information.

After collecting this information, the organization moves to step one of the risk management frameworks. It categorizes the information system being assessed and the information stored, processed, and transmitted by the system. This is usually done by performing a business impact assessment (BIA).

In step two, the organization decides on the security controls used to manage the information system's risk. The choice of control is based upon the system's categorization from step one. The organization could begin by choosing a standard baseline of controls and then adding or subtracting specific controls to tailor that baseline to the system's particular needs.

After selecting controls, the organization enters step three, where it implements the chosen controls. Then, in step four, the organization performs a control assessment to determine whether the controls were correctly implemented, are operating correctly, and whether they meet the security obligations.

After completing this assessment, the organization moves to step five to authorize the information system's operation. In the federal government, the authorization process is very formal, where a senior government official must agree to any remaining risks.

Once a system is authorized and running, the organization moves to step six of the risk assessment framework. The organization monitors the implemented security controls on an ongoing basis to ensure continued effectiveness and respond to any environmental changes accordingly. If this monitoring detects significant issues, the cycle may begin afresh.

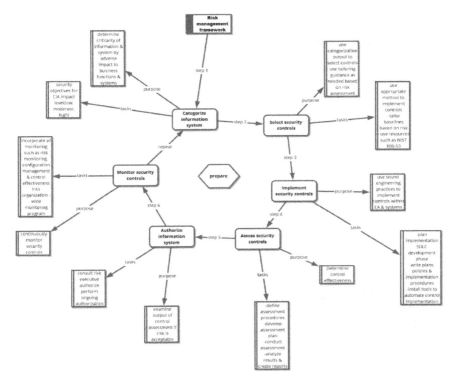

Figure 5: Risk management framework overview

Applying RMF on System development life cycle(SDLC)

Risk management framework (RMF) can be regarded as a life cycle layered on a systems development life cycle (SDLC). The steps in the SDLC are connected to RMF. The RMF produces an artifact that describes the system's specific thing or the system's risk when placed in our network.

When viewing the RMF as an overlay on the SDLC, step one starts at the SDLC development stage. This happens when an idea to develop a system is conceived. In step one, we determine the category of the system. This is based on the type of information the system will manage.

Step2 we determine which security controls to use. Here we based our selection of controls on the amount of security the system will need. The system security needs are based on what will be built into the system and the environments where it will operate.

Step 3 the security controls that have been selected are implemented or "baked in" the system.

Step 4, the system security controls are assessed by designated personnel. This assessment is done based on the specific items on a security controls matrix and determines how effective the controls control the system's information. A risk assessment report is generated. The assessment team reviews the report before it moves to the subsequent step.

Step 5 here, the risk of operating the system is made official. A review of the system and test results is done, and a formal risk assessment for the system's operation is produced. The final report states the risk rating of operating the system. For example, the risk to use the system is low or moderate, or high but can be mitigated with additional controls. The senior management then decides whether to accept the risk.

Step 6 Monitor and mitigate. The system is placed in operation, and the security controls are continuously monitored using specific tools or software that monitor and report security controls behavior. Systems can always change, or the operating can change. If step 6 reveals any vulnerabilities or the system undergoes a significant change, step 3 can be revisited, and the security controls checked before returning to step 6. In some cases, the change could trigger the system owner to review step 2, revises the system architecture, then reassess step 4. The management must be ready to protect the information or data and ensure the CIA's right levels.

The risk management framework consists of components that offer the necessary foundations and structure that an organization can use to design, implement, continuously check, supervise, critically observe and determine the status to identify any change or deviation from an expected performance level. The risk management framework also provides the foundations for reviewing and improving risk management in the enterprise. The risk management framework helps embed the necessary risk management into the entire enterprise. The framework uses the risk management process to support managing risk at various levels in its context. The framework also promotes effective risk management by ensuring that the result of the risk management process is adequately used to make informed decisions and was reported across the enterprise.

Using a risk management framework helps the organization to embed its risk management into its entire management system. Organizations should understand the components of the risk management framework and adapt them to their business needs.

Risk management framework and its components

Prominent organizations such as ISO and NIST have designed widely used risk management frameworks. These risk management frameworks are conducive for risk management, and organizations can take them and adapt them to their specific needs. An organization can choose to use a predesigned framework or build one from scratch. Irrespective of the risk management framework an organization chooses to design or implement, the key components that should be included in the framework are similar. Let us briefly discuss the essential components of a risk management framework in the next session section.

Management commitment

Management commitment is the first component of a risk management framework. Any risk management in an enterprise begins with a strong commitment from the organization's management. The management's role is vital to the success of risk management. Strategic planning is also needed to promote and get all organization levels to commit to risk management. The organization's management or leadership has to ensure that it has to design a risk management policy that aligns with the organization's culture and objectives.

Another responsibility of organizational management is to make sure that it has determined and outlined risk performance management indicators (RPI) to align with the enterprise performance indicators. Also, align the risk management goals with organizational strategies and goals. The management makes sure risk management complies with regulatory, legal, and statutory compliance. The administration also assigns roles and responsibilities, and accountabilities for risk management at all the various organizational levels and business. The management provides the needed resources for risk management. The conversation management should plan to communicate the advantages or benefits of risk management to the entire organization or stakeholders. The management continuously changes the framework to keep it relevant and suitable for the organization's needs.

Developing a risk management framework

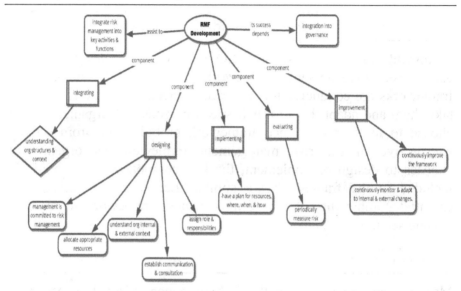

Figure 6: Overview of a risk management framework development

Organization and Context

A risk management framework is used to manage risk. The framework's design begins with a clear understanding of the internal and external environment where the organization wants to accomplish its risk management objectives. This environment is also referred to as the context. The internal and external environment can influence the framework's design. The organization must thoroughly assess the internal environment and consider the key drivers and trends that could affect its objectives. The organization also needs to consider the external environment, such as political, legal, regulatory, sociocultural, technological, economic, national, or international. External stakeholders' relationships, opinions, values, and beliefs can also influence the framework's design.

When assessing the organization's internal environment, management may consider the organizational strategies, governance responsibilities, policies, goals, culture, standards, guidelines, and contractual engagement.

Establish a risk management policy

Risk management policy is part of the risk management framework. A risk management policy constitutes the organization of intentions and direction related to risk management. The organization's leadership outlines its risk management goals or objectives and commitment in clear terms in the policy. In the policy, the administration equally discloses or addresses the organization's rationale for managing risk. The management equally finds ways to align the risk management objectives and policy to the overall organizational goals and policies. The leadership then states the responsibilities and accountabilities for managing risk within the enterprise.

Management ensures accountability

For management to be successful, management must ensure that there have countability competence and authority the managing risk. The organization also needs to implement a proper risk management process to ensure adequate and efficient controls. The management can ensure accountability by ensuring that risk owners are given the authority and responsibility to manage risk. The management will also need to identify the person responsible for developing, implementing, and maintaining the risk management framework. The organization will also be and any adequate responsibilities at various levels of the organization regarding the risk management process. The management will need to establish a performance measurement and establish appropriate conditions and structure for internal and external reporting to ensure proper recognition levels.

Resources for managing risk

For risk management to be effective, the organization will need to have the necessary resources and allocate them appropriately. When allocating resources for risk management, the organization should pay attention to the personnel, experience, and competence. The man mentioned also makes sure that there are enough resources for each stage or step of the risk management process. The organization should also consider its processes, tools, and techniques to manage risk. The organization should also ensure that they have the necessary information and knowledge management system, documented process processes, and prestigious and training programs.

Integrate risk management into the organizational processes

The risk management process should not be treated as a standalone process but integrated into its processes. When designing the overall goals of the organization processes, think about incorporating the risk management goals.

RISK MANAGEMENT PROCESS

The risk management process is a complicated and multidimensional activity that requires the participation of the whole organization. Managing risk demands a lot of commitment and responsibility. For example, the senior management has to establish the top-level goals and strategic vision for the organization. The mid-level managers plan, execute, and manage the risk-related projects while others operate the information systems that support business functions. Organizations have to establish the context for risk-based decisions or frame the risk, assess, respond to risk, and monitor the risk. Risk management requires a lot of communication and feedback, continuous improvement.

There are four main risk management process components: framing risk, assessing risk, responding to risk, and monitoring risk.

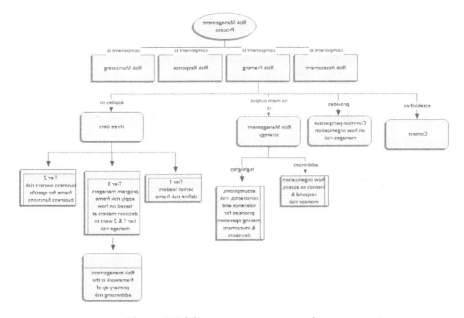

Figure 7: Risk management process's components

Multitiered risk management approach

This is an enterprise-wide risk management hierarchy. There are three tiers at which risk management should be addressed: organizational tier(tier1), business process tier(tier 2), and information systems tier (tier 3).

Tier 1

Tier 1 views risks from an organizational perspective. It provides context for all tasks related to information security management. NIST SP 800-39 tier 1 relates to the ISO 31000 risk management cycle. This tier is the foundation of listing, defining, and prioritizing the business processes required to meet its mission. Tier 1 serves the purpose of building the governance structure that oversees risk management. It determines risk tolerance, which is the level of risk or degree of certainty acceptable by the organization. It establishes and implements the organization's governance structure. The governance structure aligns with the organization's strategy, objectives, and other requirements.

The governance structure provides oversight for risk management activities. Some of the oversight activities include establishing and implementing a risk management strategy and determining rich tolerance. Oversight develops and executes investment strategies. Another significant role of the oversight for risk management activities is establishing and implementing a risk executive or function.

The risk executive serves as a shared resource for all stakeholders (managers, senior leadership) involved in the organization's risk management. The risk executive is a more comprehensive enterprise-wide approach to risk management, establishes roles and responsibilities for risk management. It ensures that risk-related activities are recognized and executed at all levels of the organization. The risk executive also provides a risk management strategy.

Risk management strategy is a document that outlines how management oversees risks. It directs how to assess, respond, and monitor risk in the enterprise. It asserts the assumptions, constraints, and trade-offs used in risk management and makes them unambiguous to everyone involved in risk management. Risk management strategy consists of risk tolerance for the organization, acceptable risk assessment methodologies, risk response strategies, and risk evaluation process across the enterprise. It aligns information security risk management activities with the organization's mission and the regulatory and legal environment. It sets the criteria for the risk management cycle activities or risk tolerance levels. Risk management strategy also ensures the proper allocation of risk management resources and monitoring of risk management activities.

Thus, in Tier 1, the tasks include risk executive (oversight and governance), the establishment of risk assessment methodologies, risk mitigation approaches, risk tolerance, and risk monitoring approaches.

Mission/Business Process (Tier 2)

Risk can only be adequately managed if associated with a relevant business process and the resources needed to execute the business processes. An organization's mission is accomplished by business processes designed to form processes that work together to achieve the organization's mission. Business processes and related resources have to be clearly defined(business process owner identified, business process owner consider possible threats to the process, consequences of those threats—this formed part of the context establishment and input to risk assessment actions.

Therefore, tier 2 risk management related activities comprise enterprise architecture, risk-aware business processes, and information security architecture. At tier 2, the risk is addressed from a business/mission perspective. From the business/mission perspective, tier 2 activities involve the design, development, and implementation of business processes that support the business functions defined at tier 1. Also, from a business/mission perspective, tier 2 activities involve guiding and informing enterprise architecture development. The enterprise architecture has information security architecture. The information security architecture provides a roadmap that defines the business-driven information security requirements and protection. The roadmap also allocates the necessary information security requirements and protection to the appropriate information systems and the environment in which the systems operate.

Information System (Tier 3)

Information systems support business processes. Information processing is done on information processing systems. There are vulnerabilities and threats concern with information processing systems. Security controls are applied to information processing systems. So, at tier 3, the organization focuses on information processing systems and their environment of operation. There is a linkage to the systems development life cycle (SDLC). Other activities include information system categorization, selection of security controls, allocation of security controls, and implementation. Other tasks at tier 3 include security control assessment, risk acceptance/authorization, and continuous monitoring.

Risk Framing or Context

Risk framing overview

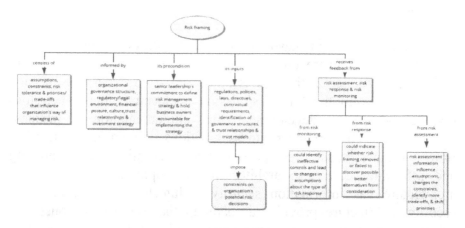

Figure 8: Summary of risk framing

Risk framing establishes the foundation for managing risk across the organization. Ricks framing defines the risks base decision boundary in the organization. It also forms step by step activities involved in the risk management process, from rick's assessment to risk response and treatment. Ricks frame produces a risk strategy. Risk strategy addresses how the organization assesses response and monitor risk. Risk strategy also exposes the organization's perceptions that are used to make risk-based decisions. Re strategy also serves as input to risk response. Risk frame requires risk assumption, constraints, priorities, and trade-offs, tolerance. Tolerance, which is the level of risk, affects all three tiers of the risk management process. Risk tolerance also affects the organization's requirements for information system provided by specific information technologies. Risks frames output includes sources in methods that I used to obtain threat information.

RISK ASSESSMENT PROCESS

RISK ASSESSMENT

Risk assessment is the process of risk identification, risk analysis, and risk evaluation. In a risk assessment, the organization identifies estimates and prioritize information security risks. Risk assessments are not a one-time activity but rather an ongoing activity because they do not provide permanent and definitive information for the organization's decision-makers. Risk assessments provide temporary information that guides and inform the courses of action for responding to information security. I used the word temporary because organizational processes and business functions can always change due to different circumstances. The risks to an organization depend on these processes or functions, vulnerabilities, threats, operating environments. If these factors that influence risk are continually changing, then it implies that the validity and usefulness of risk assessment is a function of time. In other words, the validity and effectiveness of risk assessment are time-sensitive or time-bound.

Risk assessments are used throughout all tiers in the risk management hierarchy and throughout the system development life cycle. Each assessment has a scope and purpose, which influences the resources needed for the assessment and the assessment frequency. In assessing risk, the organization or the team performing the risk assessment carefully analyzes threat and vulnerability related information to determine the extent to which events can adversely impact an organization's operations and business functions and the likelihood that those events will occur or be initiated by an adversary.

Why Risk Assessment?

There are several reasons why risk assessment is conducted. However, a fundamental risk assessment goal is to address the potential adverse impacts on enterprise-wide assets and operations, Individuals, other organizations, and even the nation. These impacts arise from the organization's usage of information systems and the information that these systems process, store, and transmit. Organizational officials are continually making risk-based decisions and activities across the three tiers of the risk management hierarchy. These risk-based and activities have to use some evidence-based information to inform the decisions made. Risk assessment results provide valuable information that supports different risk-related decisions. Risk assessment supports decisions and activities related to the design of information systems' security solutions such as information technology products, choosing appropriate security controls, authorization to use security controls, modifying specific business processes or functions for a given period or permanently. Risk assessment can also support the implementation of security solutions according to specific established requirements and the operation and maintenance of a given security solution, such as strategies to monitor the solution continuously.

Risk assessment methodology

During the risk framing, the organization defines and designs a risk management strategy. Risk methodology is part of the risk management strategy. A risk assessment methodology comprises a risk assessment process, a risk model, a risk assessment approach, and a risk analysis approach.

A risk model defines accessible risk factors and the relationship among the risk factors. **A risk approach** could be qualitative, semi-quantitative, or quantitative. A risk approach specifies the range of values the risk factor can assume while conducting a risk assessment. The risk approach also shows how the risk factors are identified, and their corresponding values combined to evaluate risk. The risk analysis approach could be vulnerability-oriented, threat oriented, asset, and impact-oriented.

The organization chooses the methodology that fits their needs. It can either choose a single or multiple risk assessment methodologies. The selection of the risk assessment methodology depends on the risk strategy and the purpose and scope. The choice of the risk methodology can also be influenced by factors such as the enterprise architecture, the system development life cycle, the time frame for any policy change, the sensitivity of the information supporting a business process or function.

CHAPTER 2: INFORMATION RISK ASSESSMENT FRAMEWORKS AND METHODOLOGIES

There are many security risk assessment frameworks out there, but companies continue to struggle with the concepts. Some popular information security risk assessment frameworks include NIST, SP 800 30, ISO31000, ISO 27005, OCTAVE, and FAIR. There seems to be a disconnect between theory and implementation. The frameworks are built on the foundational knowledge of risk. There is a need to apply the concept and principles to help the workforce truly. The practical implementation is something that is missing from the numerous frameworks. For example, how do you go about classifying your company assets and identify threats to these assets? There is a gap that exists between conceptual risk framework and workplace implementation.

This section will provide brief coverage of the significant information security risk assessment frameworks and practical ideas and techniques to implement the frameworks mentioned above' underlying principles.

WHAT IS THE FRAMEWORK?

A framework provides a logical structure or model used to organize activities or information that guide users to execute a task or series of tasks. An information security risk framework provides a logical arrangement or structure that guides users to perform risk assessment tasks. These frameworks often dwell on the theoretical details or risk-related foundational concepts, decision matrices, principles, and tiny implementation details.

The organization employs various methodologies to carry out a risk assessment. All these different methods pose challenges. Other organizations choose to design or modify the existing frameworks to come up with their custom framework. There are pros and cons of standard versus custom frameworks. One of the advantages of a custom framework is that it can be customized to meet your organization's needs and more straightforward to implement. However, a custom framework might be difficult to understand the reasons behind a customized framework rather than a standard framework.

Let us look at some high-level descriptions of major risk assessment frameworks. This briefing will give you an idea of the different frameworks you can choose from to perform security risk assessment projects.

OCTAVE METHOD

The OCTAVE® method—Operationally Critical Threat, Asset, and Vulnerability Evaluation—was created by the CERT® Survivable Enterprise Management team. The goal is to help perform information security risk assessments in context with the operational and strategic drivers they rely on to meet their mission. This OCTAVE Allegro, together with its predecessors OCTAVE and OCTAVE-S, forms a family of OCTAVE assessments. Like OCTAVE and OCTAVE-S, OCTAVE Allegro is centered on placing risk assessment in the appropriate organizational context. However, it offers an alternate method that is explicitly aimed at information assets and their resiliency. This different approach can enhance an organization's ability to position and perform the risk assessment more efficient and produce meaningful results.

OCTAVE is an approach for identifying and evaluating information security risks. It aims to help an organization to

- identify assets that are essential to the organization
- create a qualitative risk evaluation approach that describes the enterprise's operational risk tolerance
- identify vulnerabilities and threats to the organization's assets
- evaluate potential harm to the organization's assets if the threats exploit the vulnerabilities. SEI Software

The OCTAVE Method

The OCTAVE method was the first OCTAVE methodology. The OCTAVE method has an implementation guide that consists of procedures, guidelines, worksheets, and information catalogs. The OCTAVE method is implemented by an interdisciplinary team, mostly through workshops, to gather the necessary information about the company. The OCTAVE method targets large organizations that have over 300 employees, multi-layered hierarchy, computing infrastructure. The organizations also have to be capable of running their vulnerability assessments and interpreting the results. Organizations can tailor the OCTAVE method to suit their operating environment.

OCTAVE-S

The OCTVE-S was the next OCTAVE methodology after the OCTAVE method. The goal of OCTAVE-S is to bring the OCTVAVE-based approach to small organizations with less than 100 employees. OCTAVE-S consists of three phases. The main difference between OCTAVE-S and OCTAVE method is that OCTAVE-S, by a team of analysts(three to five people), has a deeper understanding of the organization's information- asset security requirements. There are no workshops involved in OCTAVE-S implementation. Also, OCTAVE-S is more structured and does not require extensive examination of the organization's infrastructure.

OCTAVE Allegro

The OCTAVE® method—Operationally Critical Threat, Asset, and Vulnerability Evaluation—was created by the CERT® Survivable Enterprise Management team. The goal is to help perform information security risk assessments in context with the operational and strategic drivers they rely on to meet their mission. This OCTAVE Allegro, together with its predecessors OCTAVE and OCTAVE-S, forms a family of OCTAVE assessments. Like OCTAVE and OCTAVE-S, OCTAVE Allegro is centered on placing risk assessment in the appropriate organizational context. However, it offers an alternate method that is explicitly aimed at information assets and their resiliency. This different approach can enhance an organization's ability to position and perform the risk assessment more efficient and produce meaningful results.

OCTAVE is an approach for identifying and evaluating information security risks. It aims to help an organization to:

- identify assets that are essential to the organization,
- create a qualitative risk evaluation approach that describes the enterprise's operational risk tolerance

- identify vulnerabilities and threats to the organization's assets
- evaluate potential harm to the organization's assets if the threats exploit the vulnerabilities. SEI Software

OCTAVE Allegro is a phased approach, which constitutes eight steps and four distinct areas of activity or phases performed during the eight steps. The activity areas include establishing drivers or risk measurement criteria, profiling the company's assets, identifying threats, and identifying and mitigating risks. The eight steps go from establishing risk management criteria, developing information asset profile, identifying information asset containers, identifying areas of concerns, identifying threat scenarios, identifying risk, analyzing risk, and finally selecting a mitigation approach. The output from each step serves as input to the next step.

OCTAVE Allegro focuses on producing the risk assessment of the organization's operational environment without requiring the analysis team to have much risk assessment knowledge. It focuses on how information asset is used, stored, transported, and processed. It equally looks at how the asset is exposed to security risks, vulnerabilities, and consequences or harm to the organization due to the threats and vulnerabilities.

Implementation of OCTAVE Allegro

Activity Areas of the OCTAVE Allegro Methodology

The first activity is to establish the organization's drivers. This is where the organization creates risk measurement criteria that are in alignment with its risk drivers. This is followed by establishing and identifying the profile asset that will be used in the risk assessment. The goal is to identify the critical assets that should be included in a risk assessment engagement. This can be done in two ways. The client (the company) already has specific assets identified in the engagement scope. The client will want you(the analysis team) to determine the critical asset included in the engagement.

SELECT THE CRITICAL ASSETS OR RESOURCES

The selection is made by considering the internet-facing services, standard infrastructure services like DNS, DHCP. The team also looks for a server supporting critical business processes, servers that store or process company sensitive information or data, desktop environment including laptops workstations and printers, network and security devices, and physical facilities.

SECURITY REQUIREMENTS

The first task is to categorize the security requirements into categories to properly assess the risk exposure of any threat and vulnerability pair. At this point, the team has already gathered enough information. It is ready to pure threat profile using one of two methods. The team can build a security profile by focusing on observed weaknesses and then modeling threats that could exploit those weaknesses or model the most likely threat and then identify any related witnesses of vulnerabilities.

THREAT PROFILES

The next activity is to identify threats to the assets and create a threat profile. A threat profile can be built using the practical weakness approach or using the most likely threat approach. The observed weakness approach is more focused and has a greater risk of missing severe issues, and it is more dependent on the assessment team's experience. The most likely threat approach produces several possibilities, and there is less risk of missing more severe issues, and it is less dependent on the assassin team's experience. It is possible to combine the two approaches starting with the observed weaknesses and then move into a most likely threat approach.

To build a threat profile for the organization, the team will have to identify the organizational information assets. The team begins by establishing the impact evaluation criteria, then identifies the assets and evaluates the organization's security patches. The team then proceeds to create the threat profiles by first selecting the critical assets, identifying their security requirements, and identifying the threats to those vital assets.

After building a threat profile, the next activity is to identify and mitigate risks. Identifying and mitigating risks involves evaluating risks and developing a security strategy.

There are two tasks in identifying and mitigating risk activity: identifying and analyzing the risks and developing protection strategy and mitigation plans. Risks evaluation involves determining the likelihood and severity of the threat and vulnerability pairs. Also, choose the risk exposure and sensitivity and determine what controls can be put in place to mitigate the risks. Then determine the residual risk level after the controls are put in place.

The second task involves developing a security strategy and mitigation plans. This is a persuasive briefing to the executive. You make recommendations for a mitigation strategy, select the mitigations steps, identify a short-term actions plan, and update any existing mitigation plan's status.

Steps of the OCTAVE Allegro Methodology

Step 1- build risk measurement criteria.

This first step involves creating the organizational drivers used to assess the impacts of risk on its business objectives. The goal is to establish a means to measure risk. A set of qualitative measures against which the impacts of identified risks can be evaluated (set of risk measurement criteria) is established and include the drivers. The most significant effect on the organization's mission and business objectives must be known and probably included in the risk frame. The recognition of the most significant impacts helps in the prioritization of impacts. For each impact area, create different impact criteria. OCTAVE recommends evaluating areas such as safety and health, financial, productivity, and fines and legal penalties. For each impact area, provide scores and ranking, which would be included in the impact score.

Step 2 Build an information asset profile.

Create a profile for the organization's information asset. A profile represents an asset and describes its features or characteristics, qualities, and value. The asset has to be clearly defined with precise boundaries and specific security requirements. Worksheets are used to present the profile of each asset. These worksheets can be used in subsequent steps to identify threats and risks. The list of the information assets collected is a function of their importance to the organization. You can use a brainstorming session to select the most vital assets. These assets are ranked based on particular benchmarks. Some essential activities performed here include documenting the asset owner, describing the critical assets, identifying the confidentiality, integrity, and availability requirements, identify the essential CIA requirement and reasons that particular asset is the most important to the organization.

Step 3 Identify the containers for information assets.

Information assets are stored, transported, and processed in different places within the organization and outside the organization. These locations constitute the container of information assets. So, asset containers are assets that have information. It is essential to identify all these containers of information assets. For example, many organizations outsource their IT services to cloud providers. These cloud providers will manage the containers that have the organization's critical information assets. The organization has to ensure the cloud provider's service level agreement includes a clear understanding of the information assets' security requirements. There are necessary controls to protect the assets and not expose them to risks. Step 3 of the OCTAVE Allegro process ensures that all the internal and external containers of information assets are identified. The identification includes mapping all the information assets to all the containers in which the information asset lives. Information collected that classified as:

Physical (such as the Data centers, the location of the data, and hardware).

Technical including hardware, type of information, processes, etc. People, including asset owners and other applicable contacts.

Step 4 Identify areas of concern and examining supporting infrastructure.

This step deals with finding various ways in which a real-world situation can threaten the organization's information. This step involves identifying weaknesses, threats, and their adverse impact on the organization's assets. There are different approaches to characterizing threats to the assets. The threat could be viewed as unique to the organization, its operating environment, or the industry to which it belongs. Examples could include identifying web application security weaknesses such as broken authentication(vulnerability).

Step 5: Identify threat scenarios

This step is where you identify a threat that can leverage an identified vulnerability to create a scenario or threat event. For example, a broken authentication for a web application could lead to unauthorized access to the application by cybercriminals (threat). The threat scenarios build statements that combine asset, access, actor, motive, and outcome. For example, what reason will drive a hacker to seek access and application and steal sensitive data(outcome)? The building of threat scenarios will lead to a "threat listing." Some people referred to this listing as a "catalog." Allegro provides a Threat Scenario Questionnaire that guides you by preparing for threat scenarios through a standardized list of questions.

Step 6: Identification of risk

Here you create a table containing a threat and vulnerability pair and the corresponding impact on an asset. The threat, vulnerability, and impact combine to produce a risk. A threat exploits a vulnerability to create an impact or consequence that leads to risk on the organization's asset.

Step 7: Risk Analysis

Risk analysis is focused solely on impact and not impact and likelihood, as in most frameworks. Likelihood or probability is considered in the risk mitigation approach. Allegro uses scoring for prioritization purposes and as an indication of the degree of risk. The score shows the relative importance of the risk. For example, if risk A has a score of 20 and risk B has a score of 8, it does mean that risk A is relatively more important than risk B.

Select the Risk Mitigation Approach

Risk is categorized using a relative risk matrix. The categorized risks could be in a different risk mitigation approach "pools." Pools occur when the risk score intersects with the likelihood of the threat emerging. There four pools where the categorized risk could fall into:

Pool 1-mitigate.

Pool 2- mitigate or defer.

Pool 3- defer or accept.

Pool 4- accept.

Once the pools are determined, they become the source of the mitigation plan. The mitigation approach in OCTAVE is very flexible.

FAIR (FACTOR ANALYSIS OF INFORMATION RISK)

FAIR is a quantitative risk analysis model that analyzes risks in financial terms. FAIR stands for the factor analysis of information risk. It does not necessarily have to apply to information risk, but the standard itself focuses on information risk.

It was published in 2005 and is actively maintained by the FAIR Institute. In 2009, The Open Group adopted it as the only international standard quantitative model for cybersecurity and operational risk.

FAIR has four steps: Identity scenarios components, Evaluate Loss Event, Evaluate Probable Loss, Derive and Articulate risk.

Within OPEN FAIR, Risk is defined as the probable frequency and probable magnitude of future loss. This definition is a crucial distinction from other frameworks. FAIR does focus on risk as a loss side of things. According to FAIR, when we talk about risk, we are focused on loss to the organization. This means that organizations can discuss risk consistently. Whether this is analysts within the same organization are trying to figure out the amount of risk they are attempting to mitigate or between organizations. By putting things in the units of currency per timeframe or probable frequency and probable magnitude, we avoid some of the confusion about potentially having a high risk depending on your personal preferences and views of risk. Thus, you could have a very different understanding of what a high risk means. For example, this allows you to present things as potentially five different losses of $2,000,000 in a single year, which will enable you to work more actively to mitigate those risks.

FAIR has added some guidance to look at the overall risk management process. They have broken down the FAIR standard guide to look at the specific activities that need to take place in those areas. For risk identification, there is a need to identify and characterize the assets, threats, and controls. Then look at the impact and loss elements.

The risk analysis phase is where we do a deep dive. Once we have made the threat identification and apply the quantitative techniques, we move to the risk management step. Get that accurate risk model to get meaningful measurements to be used if we have different scenarios. Scenarios provide those useful comparisons between the different scenarios based on those measurements and the actual quantitative guidance that we use to get the losses. These will lead to those well-informed decisions.

Risk evaluation phase where we look at the results and see how they guide the decision-making process.

According to FAIR Institute, FAIR addresses some core challenges in risk analysis and management. The primary challenge is understanding the factors that contribute to risk and the relationships between those factors.

The FAIR framework seeks to resolve the disparate terms that differ across frameworks. For example, the definition of risk, which varies among frameworks.

This framework consists of

- an ontology of risk factors and their relationships,
- methods for measuring risk driving factors,
- a standard definition of terms used to describe and measure risk,
- a measured approach to simulating the relationships such as Monte Carlo, and
- a scenario modeling approach.

It uses stages to break down its activities.

FAIR defines risk as the likely frequency and magnitude of future loss. This is referred to in the nomenclature as Loss Event Frequency (LEF) and Loss Magnitude (LM). Moreover, it can be represented by a derived value that represents loss exposure. FAIR concentrates primarily on "pure" risk resulting in a loss instead of theoretical risk (which could produce either a loss or a profit). FAIR links the probability and magnitude of a loss to an asset.

According to FAIR, an essential step in determining risk is unambiguously identifying assets and their value. An asset has intrinsic value, which creates potential liability. For example, if the company cares more about the server's data, it is labeled an asset and not the server. If the server is labeled as the primary asset, it does not lead to a precise analysis or direct strategy of the potential risk to the data itself.

There are six types of losses used to determine the Value at Risk (VaR) for an asset: productivity, response, replacement, fines and judgments, competitive advantage, and reputation. Threats are the forces that represent an ability to cause these losses actively. The threat is also referred to in the FAIR framework as "threat agents" or "threat community." FAIR analysis approach focuses on probability, not possibility, of a loss caused by a threat. The following example shows the difference between probability and possibility.

There is a 65% chance of rain between 1 pm and 4 pm today (probability).

It may rain today (possibility).

FAIR Taxonomy

The two major branches in FAIR's risk taxonomy are Loss Event Frequency (LEF) and Loss Magnitude (LM). Each branch has factors that drive the occurrence and magnitude of losses.

The FAIR framework uses "stages" to break down its activities.

The first stage is the identification of the asset at risk. An asset has value and liability. The second activity in this stage is identifying the threat community, which is the source of the threat(other frameworks refer to as threat sources/agents/factors).

Evaluating Loss Event Frequency

The second stage deals with Evaluating loss event frequency. This stage consists of five steps. Each step ends up with a value, subsequently used for some computation in the risk assessment process.

THREAT EVENT FREQUENCY (TEF) is defined as the probable frequency, within a given timeframe, that a threat agent could act against an asset and result in a loss. This seeks to answer the question: How frequently can the attack happen? FAIR uses a five-point scale with corresponding frequency ranges from high to very low. For example, it means that the TEF is greater than 100 times per year for a rating of Very High. A rating of Very Low means the TEF is less than 0.1 times per year.

THREAT CAPABILITY (TCAP) is the probable level of force that a threat can employ against an asset. This measurement is focused on the skills and resources a threat agent has available to attack an asset. The main question to answer here is: what is the attacker's capability to conduct the attack? A five-point scale is used. The scale ranges from Very High(meaning that the threat capability is at the top 2% compared against the overall threat population) to Very Low(which means the TCap is at the bottom 2% compared against the overall threat population).

ESTIMATE CONTROL STRENGTH(CS): FAIR defines CS as the expected effectiveness of controls, over a given timeframe, as measured against a baseline level of assets ability to resist compromise. The CS measures the strength of the controls in place. The control strength measurement uses a five-point scale ranging from Very High(indicates that the control protects against all but the top 2% of an average threat population) to Very Low(meaning that the control only protects against the bottom 2% of an average threat population).

DERIVE VULNERABILITY (Vuln): FAIR defines Vuln as the probability that an asset will be unable to defend or resist the threat agent's actions. As a result, the threat event will become a loss event. A vulnerability exists when there is a difference between the threat agent's attack and an asset's ability to resist that attack. To obtain Vuln value, we consider Threat capability(TCap) and Control Strength(CS). We plot a TCap versus Control Strength and find the point where the two intersect. TCap is inversely proportional to Control Strength.

DERIVE LOSS EVENT FREQUENCY (LEF). LEF is the probable frequency, within a given period, that a threat will cause harm to an asset. For example, the number of times a year hacker will perform a denial of service attack against the company website that results in loss of use for customers. The value of LEF is derived from TEF and Vuln. We plot a graph of TEF and Vuln and identify where the two intersect. LEF indicates how likely a threat source would successfully exploit a vulnerability in an asset.

Evaluating Probable Loss Magnitude (PLM)

This stage deals with evaluating the impact of the threat event occurs. It determines the severity of loss from a successful threat event. To assess the loss, we estimate the worst-case scenarios and then estimate probable loss magnitude.

Estimating the worst-case scenarios determines the threat action that would generate the worst-case outcome. FAIR provides a loss form table that could be used to determine the magnitude of the loss.

Next, we estimate the probable loss magnitude. FAIR defines PLM as the most likely threat community's actions. Most likely indicates that the event might have the greatest probability to occur as compared to a worst-case scenario. For PLM, we add the loss magnitudes to get the overall magnitude.

Derive Risk

Deriving and articulating entails plotting the Loss Event Frequency (LEF) and the Probable Loss Magnitude (PLM). The intersection of LEF and PLM gives the final risk score.

FAIR risk assessment results focus on the most likely and maximum values., generously rounding off the results to whole numbers. The results of a FAIR risk assessment are often created in a tabular layout.

Other concepts to understand from the FAIR include Contact Frequency (CF). CF is the probable frequency, within a timeframe, that a threat will come into contact with an asset. Contact can be physical or "logical" (e.g., over the network).

Probability of Action (PoA) is the probability that a threat will act against an asset once contact occurs. Once contact occurs between a threat and an asset, action against the asset may or may not happen.

Difficulty measures the strength of control compared to the level of effort attacks require for a successful breach. An online system that leverages multi-factor authentication and VPN has a more incredible difficulty to a threat community than one secured by a simple username and password pair and no VPN.

Loss Magnitude (LM) is the probable magnitude of loss stemming from a loss event.

Primary loss is the direct result of a threat's actions upon an asset and every so often embodies the intention of acting against the asset. The owner of the involved assets is deemed the primary stakeholder in an analysis.

A secondary risk is a result of secondary stakeholders, such as customers, stockholders, regulators, etc., responding disapprovingly to the primary loss event. This reaction could result in an additional loss to the primary stakeholder. An example is regulators fining a company after a data breach.

ISO 27005

In the ISO 2700 series, the part that deals with risk management are covered in ISO 27005. There exists an ISO standard for risk management, which is ISO 31000. ISO 27005 is an adaptation of ISO 31000 in the context of information security. ISO 27005 is in line with the risk management requirements present in ISO 27001. As we will discuss later in this section, risk management is an essential component of ISO 27001.

ISO 27005 contains Information security risk techniques for information security management. It focuses on providing the information security risk management processes necessary to implement the information security management systems(ISMS) in ISO 27001. ISO 27005 was published by the International Organization for Standardization (ISO) and the International Electrotechnical Commission(IEC).

ISO 27005 is a risk assessment guidance and does not recommend any risk assessment methodologies. ISO 27005 can be applied to organizations of different types and aligns with NIST SP 800-30. In terms of its workflow, ISO27005 supports an iterative approach to risk assessment. In other words, it describes an ongoing information security risk assessment process. The five steps of this process are:

- Context Establishment
- Information security risk assessment.
- Information security risk treatment.
- Information security risk communication.
- Information security monitoring and review

Let us look at the five steps in detail.

Establish the risk management context:

To establish the risk assessment framework, we have to determine the following elements:

Scope: Define the scope of the risk assessment

For example, we might want to limit the analysis to assets that are specific to a particular activity or function within an organization

List the compliance requirements: such as the regulations, laws that apply, and also contractual obligations that have been signed.

Method(s) to be used: As we have mentioned earlier, ISO 27005 is not a risk assessment method per se. It is instead a guide that enumerates the essential steps of the risk management process. We will therefore have to specify the way we intend to use among the various existing methods. There are methods such as CRAMM, OCTAVE, or EBIOS. We will discuss them later.

Risk Assessment

Risk assessment in ISO27005 is done in three steps: Risk Identification, Risk Analysis or estimation, and Risk Evaluation.

Asset Identification

Identify assets in scope for the risk assessment. Within the scope determined in step 1, we do an inventory of all assets in scope. In ISO 27005, assets can either be primary or secondary. "Primary assets" are the core processes and information, while "secondary or supporting" asset includes hardware, software, personnel, structure, site, and network. The asset types are found in Annex B of the ISO 27005 standards document.

These assets could be tangible, such as workstations, or intangible such as data files. This inventory includes "primary assets," which means information assets and business processes(functions). We also find among the assets "supporting or secondary assets" such as networks, software, hardware, people, facilities, etc.

In ISO27005, we need to determine the importance of these identified assets in terms of confidentiality, integrity, and availability. The essential assets that are "information" and "functions" have security requirements or needs according to the three criteria of confidentiality/integrity/ Availability. For example, we perform a risk assessment for an expense management system. In this system, we identify information assets, such as:

- Information:

- Personally, identifiable information (First name. last name, address, etc.)
- Bank account information
- Travel summary
- Functions: we also identify business processes such as
- Expense report entry
- Expense report approval
- Reimbursement
- Supporting assets: we find supporting assets, such as:
- An expense management application
- A network of interconnections
- Workstations

We use a matrix to associate these different elements. For example, we find the bank account numbers on the database server and some workstations.

Identification of Security Threats

The goal is to compile a listing of potential threats to the identified assets. Asset owners, facilities management, users, human resource department could help in the threat identification. Other sources of threat identification could be previous incident reports. ISO27005 has included a recommended threat catalog found in Annex C.

We identify the different threats to these assets that should be taken into consideration. A threat has the potential to cause harm to the assets. Threats can be identified with the help of different stakeholders. The stakeholders could be internal or external to the organization, such as asset owners, users of the assets, administrative staff, information security personnel, legal team members, insurance companies, or government authorities. Threats could include theft, failure, denial of service attacks, natural disasters, etc. At this stage, we try to compile a list of possible and relevant scenarios.

Identification of existing security controls.

The goal is to identify the existing and planned controls. However, ISO27005 does not prescribe an identification method. It provides some references for information sources that could assist in conducting the identification of existing controls. Some sources include on-site reviews, documents containing information about controls, internal audit results, and information security staff.

We identify the existing controls that the organization has put in place to avoid unnecessary costs or work or risk. We also include controls that have already being planned for implementation.

Identification of vulnerabilities.

The objective is to identify vulnerabilities for the identified assets. Examples of vulnerabilities are found in Annex D of the standard. ISO27005 has also provided information sources that can be used for the identification of vulnerabilities. Some of the information sources include interviews, Document analysis, Questionnaires, Code reviews, Vulnerability scanning, penetration testing reports, and physical inspection.

We determine the vulnerabilities that are specific to the identified assets or assets already inventoried. In the context of risk management, vulnerabilities are essentially the characteristics that increase risk in the face of threats. Threats exploit these vulnerabilities to produce risk. For example, consider a hotel building where windows are at street level or in the street's dark end. The presence of windows at the street level may be regarded as a vulnerability. This vulnerability increases the risk of threats of vandalism or burglary.

Identification of damage or consequences.

The goal is to determine the possible consequences or harm That "an incident scenario" (also referred to as threat scenario in other frameworks) causes. In terms of impact analysis, ISO27005 uses a more quantitative approach. It provides a list of risk factors that could be employed to identify and measure consequences or harm to the assets. ISO has provided quantitative aspects of impact(such as financial loss or cost to replace an asset, cost of interruption of service, or suspension of operations) in Annex C.

An organization determines the impacts of the incident scenarios (identified and listed) in terms of investigation and repair costs, lost work time, lost opportunities, health and safety at work, expenses, fees, purchase of equipment, and impact on reputation and image. After determining the impacts of the different incident scenarios, they conduct a risk assessment. That means to estimate the impact on the company.

Risk Estimation

Risk estimation has three main actions: Assessment of consequences, Assessment of incident likelihood, and measure of the risk level.

Assessment of consequences or harm: This activity aims to assess what an incident scenario causes an asset. The standard recommends that the following consequences be evaluated: opportunity lost, work time lost, investigation and repair time, image reputation and goodwill, the financial cost of specific skills to repair the damage, and health and safety. These consequences are subdivided into direct and indirect impacts in Annex B.

Assessment of incident likelihood: This activity aims to use qualitative and quantitative estimation techniques to assess an incident scenario's likelihood. ISO27005 recommends that the following factors should be considered while conducting the likelihood assessment:

- Vulnerabilities
- Frequency of occurrence of the threat
- Threat source's motivation and capability
- Geographical factors and the environment
- Existing controls

Estimating the risk level: This activity aims to compute the values for likelihood and consequences and use those values to calculate the risk value. There are risk estimation approaches in Annex E of ISO27005, which provide the computation matrices and tables for calculating risk as a function of likelihood and consequences.

Risk Evaluation

There is no standard method for scoring threat, impact, and risk. You can choose to evaluate it qualitatively (based on subjective measurements, such as 'moderate,' 'severe,' 'low,' etc.) or quantitatively (based on absolute measurements, such as a mathematical calculation).

The risk value assessment can also be qualitative. For example, we are using a "low/medium/high" impact value Or quantitative with real costs in dollar amount, for instance, to represent potential losses.

Both the qualitative and quantitative approaches have pros and cons. A qualitative method for risk value is usually more intuitive but also very flexible. It fits any scenario. Some people say it is the only possible approach when no quantitative data is available.

A quantitative approach can facilitate management decision-making because it provides an analysis of costs versus benefits and helps compare the potential return on investment of different risk treatment scenarios. The impact value usually depends on the value and criticality of the affected asset by the incident scenario. It is essential to consider, for example, the asset replacement cost, the acquisition and configuration cost of the new asset if the affected asset is replaced. We do not forget the cost of interruption of operations during the incident.

Incident probability assessment: For the various threat incident scenarios identified, we then estimate the probability of the threat occurring or "probability of occurrence."

Risk level assessment: Once we have established a list of the potential threat incidents, we assess the risk associated with each threat incident. The risk level depends on the probability of the threat occurring and the impact level if the threat occurs.

Risk prioritization: All the identified risks with risk score or value will be ranked in descending order of risk level. This risk prioritization gives a hierarchical inventory of potential threat scenarios. The risk assessment determines which risks will be given priority.

Risk treatment options: For the different identified risks, the organization has to choose one of the four possible treatment options:

Avoidance

The organization can decide to avoid the risk. In this case, the risk is considered to be too high. As a result, the activity that leads to the risk will be discontinued. For example, suppose the organization was considering launching a new application, assessing, and realizing that the risk level is very high. In that case, the company can decide to avoid the risk by canceling its launch.

Reduction

The second option for risk treatment is to reduce the risk. The organization considers the effort to reduce the risk level to a bearable or acceptable level. In other words, controls will be implemented to reduce the impact or probability of the threat.

Transfer

The organization can also transfer risk to another entity that can manage it, such as an insurance company or a subcontractor.

Acceptance

Finally, the risk can be accepted by the organization. They decide to do nothing and leave things the way they are. The decision to leave things they are could be because the risk is low or the costs of treating the risk are too high.

These are the four possible risk treatment options: avoid, reduce, transfer, or accept the risk. For each risk identified during the risk analysis, we have to choose one of these options.

Risk treatment plan

Once the organization has decided regarding risk treatment, the activities needed to implement these decisions must be identified and planned. Priority actions will be defined to ensure that activities are focused on the highest risks.

For example, see the *table 11*.

Table 11: risk treatment plan

Risk	Risk level	Prio rity	Treat ment	Action details	Necess ary resourc es	Person (s) in charge	Begin/ End
Unautho rized users can connect via the extranet to SharePo int and read sensitive files with the guest ID	High	Hig h	Avoi dance	Make ShareP oint availab le and imple ment access control	10 hours to reconfi gure and test the system	Jeff Vangel ShareP oint admin, Adul Shaffe r firewal l admin	03/21/ 2021 03/23/ 2021

Risk communication

Stakeholders and decision-makers have to be informed through the risk assessment process. This constant communication helps to limit any misunderstandings with decision-makers and to get them involved with the responsibility.

The risk treatment plan's acceptance of the risk treatment plan must be submitted to management for approval. Once the management has approved the treatment plan, they must allocate the needed resources to implement it.

Residual risk is the that remains after controls have been implemented. It is hence a "mitigated" risk. Residual risks must be understood, accepted, and approved by management.

Risk has to be monitored and periodically reviewed. This ensures that the process remains relevant and appropriate and adapted to security objectives. The organization has to identify any changes requiring a reassessment of risk, new threats, and vulnerabilities. New threats and vulnerabilities have to be done regularly. For instance, annually.

To summarize the different steps described in ISO 27005, the first step is to define the scope of the risk assessment. Then, we conduct a risk analysis. Based on the risk analysis results, for each risk identified, we select one of the four risk treatment options available, avoid, transfer, reduce, or accept risk). Once an option is chosen, there may be a residual risk to deal with. We then decide whether the residual risk is acceptable or not. If it is acceptable, we are done. If it is not acceptable, a new risk management strategy would be defined.

Also, ISO 27005 standard is based on the "Plan-Do-Check-Act" principle. Plan-Do-Check-Act is the famous Deming's wheel that is the continuous improvement cycle. We start by planning, and then things are done based on what was planned, then we check to ensure that we did what was planned, and finally we take into account and correct any errors, deviations, etc., to feed a new phase of planning. Moreover, we are back at the beginning of the cycle. Thus, in ISO 27005, we will not assess the risks just once and be done, but it will be done periodically. For example, we do a risk assessment twice a year, risk treatment, and how risks were treated in the previous cycle. This puts us in a cyclical pattern of continuous improvement.

As we mentioned earlier, ISO 27005 is not a risk analysis method per se, instead of a reference guide. We will have to select an appropriate method to conduct a risk analysis. The fundamental principle of these methods is that if different persons perform the same analysis using the same methodology, they should obtain similar results.

OCTAVE (Operationally Critical Threat and Vulnerability Evaluation) Method. OCTAVE method is structured in three phases: Security needs profiling, vulnerability assessment, security strategy, and plan development. OCTAVE is described in a previous section.

The CRAMM(CCTA Risk Analysis and Management Method).

The CRAMM method is structured in 3 phases: the definition of the assets at risk, the analysis of risks and vulnerability, and the definition and choice of security controls.

Then there is the MICROSOFT Risk Management Guide. This guide has four main phases: risk assessment, decision support, implementation of security controls, and program effectiveness measurement.

TRA(Threat and Risk Assessment).

The TRA methodology includes four steps.

- establish the scope (i.e.,
- identify the employees and assets to be safeguard or backed up),
- determine the threats and assess the probability and impact of their occurrence,
- assess the vulnerabilities according to the accuracy of the safeguards and computerize the risk, and
- Implement additional safeguards, if necessary, to reduce the risk to an acceptable level.

NIST 800-30

NIST SP800-30 provides a basis or foundation for the development of an effective risk management program. It contains the definitions and practical guidance needed to assess and mitigate the risks identified in IT systems.

EBIOS (Expression of Needs and Identification of Security Objectives) method.

It has five steps: circumstantial study(determine the context), security requirements, risk study, identification of security goals, and security requirements.

MEHARI(Method for Harmonized Analysis of Risk) Method.

This method starts with an audit of the vulnerabilities of the information system. The risk analysis is then conducted based on the findings of the audit.

Other methods include SIEMENS, RCMP, ANSSI, CLUSIF, CERT.

This is not an exhaustive list. You could choose another method that is more suitable for your organizational needs.

The process described in ISO 27005 lists the steps essential for the risk management process, adding a continuous improvement logic.

Risk assessment has several steps. These steps include preparing for the risk assessment, conducting the risk assessment, Communicate the results of the risk assessment, and treatment maintain the risk assessment. There are several activities involved at each step of the risk assessment. The figure shows the essential activities of information risk assessment in the sections that the author will provide for each activity. The author will then leverage the NIST 800-30, ISO3100 & ISO 31010 to discuss the detailed tasks involved in risk assessment.

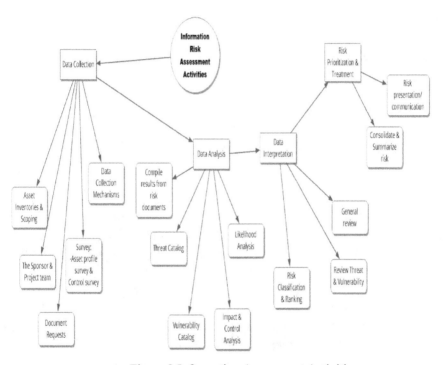

Figure 9:Information Assessment Activities

ACTIVITIES INVOLVED IN RISK ASSESSMENT.

This section of risk assessment will not be based on a single framework but draws information from various frameworks. This approach will use common denominators from the frameworks. For example, all the frameworks involve risk determination, identification of threats, components of risk, etc.

The main stages in the information security risk assessment are:

Data Collection,

Data Analysis,

Risk Analysis,

Reporting and

Maintenance.

These stages are typical in most risk assessment frameworks.

These stages have been discussed in detail in the risk assessment preparation section. Let us briefly summarize each stage here.

DATA COLLECTION

The data collection is where we should begin our risk assessment engagement. Data provides the necessary support for our analysis. The different business units within the organization should be included in the risk assessment process. Some of the activities that go into data collection include finding the organization's right project sponsor, aligning the risk assessment with the organization's strategic objectives by interviewing top executives in the company. The data collection stage activities are to assemble asset inventories with their respective asset owners, interview the asset owners, and put together the various IT resources with their security controls. Once the asset inventories are in place, we proceed to data analysis.

Data Analysis

We have collected many data about the assets, their owners, the business functions they support, the various controls, and technical contacts. This information can be stored in a spreadsheet. However, at this point, we might have all the needed data. There are situations where data might come in a month into a project that is supposed to last for just two months. That is the real-life engagements. However, while waiting for the data to come in, we begin to analyze what we have so far. We start reviewing the previous security risk assessment reports(SAR). We also review risks and controls, security metrics. Prepare threat and vulnerability pair listings, perform impact analysis plan, design, perform likelihood analysis and control analysis plan, and prepare risk assessment scale(qualitative, semi-quantitative, or quantitative).

We automate the analysis plans and computations using spreadsheets, databases, or other tools. At the end of the analysis, we produce risk assessment templates in spreadsheets, databases, or some tool. The tool has a list of each reviewed asset, threats and vulnerability pairs for each asset, impacts, likelihood, control, risk ratings, and save as templates, which can then be recreated across all assets.

RISK ANALYSIS AND PRIORITIZATION

This stage involves brainstorming, discussing to come up with the findings of the assessment. The activities here revolve around prioritizing the risks of the critical assets, preparing controls recommendations, consulting with the teams, getting feedback, using the feedback to validate, and adjusting the results, and preparing organizational level findings and statistics. Risk treatment could also be considered at this stage.

RISK ASSESSMENT REPORT

This report is the stage where the risk assessment work is summarized into a few executive summary pages presented to executive management. There will also be a more detailed report to corroborate your results. Thus, the activities at this stage include preparing an executive management's risk assessment memo report, prepare a thorough risk assessment report, prepare supplemental material (such as Appendices), and do a debrief.

MAINTENANCE

The risk assessment process is challenging, and there is always some room for improvement in the process. In this stage, the activities are aimed at making the risk assessment experience better. Some of the activities include discussing the lessons learned, keep updated about any changes that can affect risk, and defend your risk assessment from people with different views and opinions on the risk assessment findings and conclusions.

CASE STUDY: INFORMATION SECURITY RISK ASSESSMENT OF LIONSWEB INC.

We will conduct a "high-level" quick information security risk assessment of our fictitious company called LionsWeb Inc. LionsWeb company is a multinational company specializing in conducting scientific research in the agricultural area. The risk assessment engagement is for two months, starting on October 1st.

Our team members (James and Julie) know much about the security risk assessment theory and concepts but minimal experience in conducting an end-to-end risk assessment from scratch. The team calls a few people to pick their brains on how to run a risk assessment. First, James and Julie wanted to choose which framework to use. The team first called a Chief Information Security Officer (CISO) who works for a Contractor for the US Federal Agency. Of course, the CISO recommends the NIST SP 800-30 and highlights that the NIST framework is flexible and can be adapted to fit the company's needs. Also, NIST offers principles including theory and concepts such as elements to pay attention to when assessing risk. However, it does not tell you how to encapsulate those activities or features in a project. One key thing the team from talking to the CISO was to ensure that they collect information from the entire LionsWeb company.

The team, after further conversations with several information security professionals from different industries, they realized that:

- Most people do not use any framework. Based on their industry, they might just read about security requirements and different frameworks and do things the way they see fit.

- Whatever they choose, they should make it simple. Successful implementation of a risk assessment calls for project planning and management.

The team finally decided to start the project using an established methodology. The methodology consisted of data collection, data analysis, risk analysis, risk assessment report, and risk assessment maintenance.

THE MAIN STAGES IN OUR LIONSWEB COMPANY RISK

Assessment Methodology

Data Collection at LionsWeb Company

Before performing LionsWeb's risk analysis, the team needed to obtain data to support their analysis. We include the following LionsWeb business units in the risk assessment: Information Technology(IT), Internal Audit, finance and Accounting, Research and Development, and Human Resource (HR). The activities that we consider at this stage are:

Identify the project sponsor: The project sponsor was the Head of the Internal Audit Department. The next activity is to assemble asset inventories, identify and interview asset owners and technical contacts, and review systems and security control resources.

Data collection is a rigorous activity in the risk assessment project. The team put together a plan which includes coordinating with people in the company and having appropriate communication. Their plan includes having a strong executive sponsor, having regular follow-up conversations with involved personnel, establishing strong relationships with system or asset owners, scoping the asset carefully, using different means to collect data, and using a NIST 800 53 and ISO

27002 as their standard control frameworks. Their output for data collection would be a data container(referred to as LW Data Container). LW Data container had the following information:

- Name of system or asset
- System owner
- Business function the system supports.
- Controls in place

They also identify and agree on the sponsor. The sponsor was an executive who would be the person they ultimately report to and support them throughout the project. A project sponsor should have direct access to the top management of the company, be at the executive level of the company, and be able to make high-level decisions, and be knowledgeable about audits. We think from experience that a sponsor with healthy people skills is very critical. The sponsor should be able to reach out to the company's personnel and get favorable. Without a strong sponsor, it becomes difficult for an assessment to reach out and request documents or schedule interviews.

This is mainly for an external assessment team that the company's personnel are not used to. The relationship between the team and the company's personnel might become more cordial as time goes on. However, it could be rocky(due to skepticism of team by personnel) at the beginning of the project.

The team has identified their sponsor they set up a meeting with the sponsor—the plan of the discussion centered around outlining the sponsor's responsibilities and the team's expectations. The sponsor's prominent roles are to review and approve the risk assessment approach, provide needed resources for the project, send out communications to top management and other personnel, review findings, and offer feedback.

Let us say a few words about the team. This risk assessment project was made up of two people, Julie Snow and James D. Duncan. The project team's size varies depending on different circumstances such as available personnel, size, and complexity of the project(number of assets in scope, the complexity of assessment and data collection), and time constraints.

The team had minimal experience in conducting an information risk assessment. As you might guess, this was going to be an uphill task for Julie and James. They certainly needed more help. To make matters worse for Julie and James, this was the first risk assessment that focused on remote work that the LionsWeb was conducting. It is no surprise that the team was going to face some challenges. Some of the obstacles included difficulty tracing resources such as documents and reports, creating tools for collecting and analyzing the data, rejection or challenges of their methodology, preparing a useful assessment report, meeting deadlines, and interacting with individuals and business units or departments. The team did face frustrations and sleepless nights because of specific issues such as not getting the needed documents on time.

Part of the data collection activity is to have scheduling and deadlines for crucial activities. The overall deadline to complete the whole project might be set before the project even begins. So, the team might have very little control over setting the deadline for the entire project. For the LionsWeb risk assessment project, the team was given two months to complete the project.

DATA COLLECTION MECHANISMS FOR LIONSWEB COMPANY

The team needed to have a structured and streamlined data collection process. This would help maintain consistency and provide evidence for their findings. Evidence will help defend their findings to those who might want to challenge those findings. The team divided their data collection into two groups: collectors and containers.

Collectors provide the means to get data from the source. Some data collectors that used included surveys, document request lists, interviews, and workshops. Containers store the data that is collected. The team collected many data. Some of the data collected included vulnerability assessment reports, various audit reports (such as cloud computing, IT governance), previous security risk assessment reports, system profiles, etc.

The team's containers were in the spreadsheet form. However, containers could also be in different forms, such as databases, paper documents, etc. Each container form has its advantages and disadvantages. The choice of the form of container used to store collected data depends on what the team feels comfortable using. The team has to structure and organize to be easier to retrieve and use when needed. Some common approach that has been articulated by others include collecting the data into four containers, namely: findings container, assets container, risk container, reference data container. Each container has a clear description of the data collected, a finding statement, the asset's name, the source of the data collected, the risk rating, the status of the action taken on the risk, and the system affected by the risk.

The asset container comprises data elements about the reviewed assets. The asset container contains information about the asset, such as the asset's name, asset category, asset profile, and information about the asset's controls.

The risk container holds information related to risks such as the asset's name, the threat and vulnerability pair for the asset, the impact rating or score, likelihood rating, control, and overall risk rating.

The team requested most of the documentation through the sponsor. The sponsor sent emails to the asset owner requesting specific documents. The sponsor and the IT department also created a Microsoft Teams accounted for the project and added Julie and James (the risk assessment team members). The Microsoft Teams served as the platform for sharing any requested or needed files, asking questions, etc. We think this was a very efficient communication because documents could easily be shared between the sponsor and the team and other company stakeholders involved in the project like the IT department head.

The assessment team also used surveys to collect information. The surveys were generated using online tools like SurveyMonkey, QwikSurveys, etc. They put more effort into designing the survey to ensure that it produced the needed results or valuable data. It is vital to make the survey's objective very clear to the responders or recipients; else, they might ignore the survey. The team also used interviews to collect data. Interviews are better than surveys because there is more interaction between the interviewer and interviewee. During the interview, the interviewer can ask follow-up questions, explain the process, provide more clarifications about the questions, seek more clarifications, and confirm interviewees' answers. In situations where there are many people to interview, workshops could be used. Workshops help gather the views of many people at the same time on a particular subject.

The team interviewed three executives (most C-level executives and VPs) to get their perspectives and opinions on the organization's strategic goals and risks. Though the team had wanted to interview more than three members, it was not possible because most of the executives contacted did not have time to meet with the team. However, the team could send a survey to the other executive interviewees who were not available for the interview.

The team's goal for the interview was to align the risks with the organization's mission and objectives. For example, at LionsWeb, executive management is concerned about security risks related to the disclosure of sensitive and proprietary information. Any realized security risk associated with the compromise of scientific research data is what keeps the executive up at night. LionsWeb is heavy on conducting research. The team explained the purpose of the risk assessment clearly to the executives to gain their support. Before the interview, the team researched and understood the mission and vision of the LionsWeb. They also studied the executives' background and their departments. This background information can be obtained from professional sites like LinkedIn and the project sponsor, who mostly know who the executives are. The team also prepared a brief explanation of the risk assessment objectives and an overview of the executives' methodology during the interview.

During the interview, the team questions the executives centered around the role of security in the delivery of LionsWeb's mission and how security helps achieve the company's goals. The questions were non-technical, high level, and focus on the strategic aspect of security. There are sample questions on the web that you can choose and customize to fit your needs. The questions you ask should address the organization's mission objectives, the organization's critical assets that need the most protection, the importance of security in their department, and the level of security awareness in their department. The information obtained from this interview helped the team throughout the risk assessment process. For example, it allowed the team to fit risk assessment into the organization's mission.

Document Requests from the Assessment Team

Earlier in the data collection stage, the team prepared a list of documents needed to complete the information security risk assessment project. The first thing they did was to locate the document owner and their department or location. Some of the documents on the list included previous Audit Reports, Security Assessment Risk Assessment, IT Risk Assessments, Penetration Testing Reports, Current Security Policies, Business Impact Assessment, Business Continuity, and Disaster Recovery Plans, Asset Inventories, Vendor Security Accreditation Documents, etc. Some of the documents requested did not exist, while some were not available for some reason. The team sent the document request to particular individuals that the team deemed were most likely to have the requested information.

The next task for the team was to compile the asset inventories and asset owners. The compilation of the asset inventories is usually done early during the data collection stage. Good knowledge about the IT asset and the business functions, and the company mission helps conduct interviews, surveys, requesting the necessary documents.

An asset inventory consists of a list of all the IT assets that support the various organization's business functions and processes. The team identified the systems and then later narrow them down to the most critical scoping phase. The team had some challenges in putting together the asset inventories because LionsWeb never had any. The IT assets were all over the place. The team began by identifying sources where they could get some information about the IT systems. For example, the team worked with the IT department head to locate most of the IT assets. Since there was no repository where the IT assets were stored, the team had to build a list of groups in the company that usually keep a simplified listing of applications and other IT resources. Some of the groups include It operations, network, heads of departments, enterprise architecture, asset management, finance, etc. Within these groups, the team had to identify individuals most likely to use these IT assets for operations. These individuals are the ones who know the day-to-day operational details of the assets.

In the end, the team was able to collect information such as the system diagrams, software, and hardware inventory, listings of all cloud computing tools such as web conference tools(Zoom, MS Teams, Skype), Cloud storage (OneDrive, Google Drive, etc.). The team's essential data elements were the asset name, business process it supports, description, IP address or hostname, system owner, and any technical contact. However, the team was not able to get all the assets they wanted.

Identification of Asset Characteristics and its Environment

The next task was for the team to characterize the asset(Asset Profile survey). The challenge here is that LionsWeb had so many applications that departments for their business processes. The team had to do some scoping or prioritization, which involves narrowing down the asset list to process the critical ones. The team used interviews to choose which assets were in-scope. The team talked to the prominent people familiar with the applications, telling them which asset was the most critical to the organization.

Other ways can be used to choose the in-scope assets. These ways include business impact analysis, asset scoping workshops, and critical success factor analysis. Once the team had identified the in-scope IT assets, they characterized the assets or built a profile for assessing the assets. The team assembled as much relevant information about the asset as possible. The team used surveys to gather this information. The further used post-survey interview with the system owners to validate their answers to the surveys. The team asked for information about the system itself and the environment hosting the system. The sample information collected (system profile) include:

System name,

system description,

vendor,

platform(e.g., the operating system),

system owner,

data classification(confidential, public, internal, PII, protected health information),

how the application is accessed(accessibility- remote, public, internal only),

location of the system,

data flow(how data is transmitted- HTTP, HTTPS, SFTP, FTP, removable media, etc.),

users(how many users),

user profile(who has access),

security incident(any instance of security incident), security tests performed.

Identify the system owner and technical contact and ask them about the controls on the system. Use surveys to collect information. Verify the accuracy of the information collected. The goal is to identify security controls on the particular system. Controls to look for depending on the security standards that the organization uses. If the organization has any, use the standard ones such as ISO 27001, NIST 800-53. It is vital to prioritize and rationalize the controls because you cannot review all the system controls. Create a minimum baseline of controls to review by choosing system-specific controls from the organization's published standard. Basic controls to consider by the team include data protection, patch and vulnerability management, malicious code security, Access control and authentication, security configuration, security awareness, network, auditing, physical controls, backup and disaster recovery, operational controls, etc. Respondents can measure the controls using a scale(like the Capability Maturity Model) or a yes or no.

Summary of Data Collection for LionsWeb Risk Assessment Project

The team has gathered a tone of information, and now it is time to bring all of it together in a central repository to enable efficient analysis. At this point, the team has the results from asset profile surveys, and security controls surveys, document request lists, and transcripts or notes from interviews. Their next task was to put it together. They extracted the survey results from SharePoint into a single file. Then, since they were more comfortable using Microsoft Excel, they put this data into a spreadsheet to have an aggregated single view. This consolidated and normalized view helped them become more flexible and efficient during the data analysis phase or stage. The consolidated view also makes it easier to update the data, obtain overall statistics, and efficiently use the data for references.

Analysis of the data collected

At this stage, a fair amount of data has been collected consolidated into a single view in a Spreadsheet. In this stage, the team has to compile the observations from the documents, prepare threat and vulnerability listings, compute system risk, design the control analysis, design likelihood or probability plan, and compute the final risk score. This stage's primary goal is to summarize the information collected in a form or format that will enable the team to make reasonable risk-based findings and conclusions based on the data. You can make findings and conclusions using different approaches or techniques. Some standard methods include decision matrices, formulas applying computations to the collected data. If you are using a risk framework, it will affect the data analysis technique's choice. The outcome of data analysis is the results of data computations. The team decided to use some ideas from the NIST framework to guide its risk computation. The NIST framework is flexible, and the team could tweak it to meet their needs.

Compile Observations from security-related documents

The team read through each collected document and make notes. Annotated their observations using common terminology as they perused the records—captured issues with the same root cause. For example, data protection issues are due to the absence of a data loss prevention system. They went through all the documents and collected information or observation in a standardized format. In this project, the team used Spreadsheet as their container of choice to maintain consistency. At the end of this task, they had their observation document, which contains a brief description of the finding or observation, including cause, control or mitigation, relevant information from surveys/interviews, and risk. They also mapped their observation to the assessment category (such as awareness training, application security, etc.) and indicated the finding's source, and finally identified observations with security implications to the organization.

Prepare Threat and Vulnerability Lists

Threats and vulnerabilities are essential in determining the risk of any organization's asset. The first task here is to identify and generate a listing of potential threats to the assets. Threats that include threat actors or sources (e.g., hackers), threat events, or actions taken perpetrated by threat sources could harm the organization's assets. We begin identifying threats by perusing standard threat listings to find those relevant to our organization. The team similarly approached this task. They perused the following threat listings

- the Verizon Threat Report,

- National Institute of Standards & Technology (NIST) SP 800-30: Provides about 100 threat events due to its conversation of the NIST risk analysis process.

- European Union Agency for Network and Information Security (ENISA) Threat Taxonomy: Offers a classification of threat categories and 170 threats at different detail levels.

- Bundesamt fur Sicherheit in der Informatiionstechnik (BSI) IT-GrundschutKatalog: Provides a comprehensive list of 370 threats along with a discussion and examples for each.

- International Organization for Standardization (ISO) 27005: Provides a list of about four dozen threats.

Most of the threats can be organized to have information about the type of threat source or agent (adversarial or non-adversarial), the threat event, or action. The team built its list of threats by choosing those applied to its identified systems or assets. The next task is to create a list of vulnerabilities that threat sources can exploit to produce threat events/actions that can lead to risk, and risk could adversely impact the organization. We can build vulnerabilities currently available in the organization or create some theoretical vulnerabilities that we believe could affect the organization in the future. We could combine the two. For the LionsWeb risk assessment project, the team decided to focus on the current vulnerabilities. They used the vulnerability scan results to build their list of existing vulnerabilities.

Pair the threat with the vulnerability

Now that we have identified threats and vulnerabilities, we can match the vulnerabilities to create a threat-vulnerability pair matrix. The team used a spreadsheet to generate this matrix where they put the threat source and threat event in one column and vulnerabilities in another. Threat-vulnerability match could be a one-to-many relationship where one threat matches multiple vulnerabilities.

Determining the impact

The team has identified the assets, threats, vulnerabilities. It is now time for them to build their plan for impact analysis. The first task is to have a plan that provides a repeatable process for determining the impact. Impact determination can be done in different methods (such as qualitative, semi-quantitative, or quantitative). No matter the method is chosen, we have to use a consistent way of assigning a rating to the impact. To compute the impact, we consider the data elements that provide a reliable, consistent, and repeatable value for confidentiality, integrity, and availability. For example,

Data element for confidentiality is the asset's data classification rating (how sensitive the stored, transmitted, or processed by the asset. A confidentiality determination matrix can be used to assist the team. Depending on the company, the determination matrix can vary significantly. Whatever you choose to use, ensure that the impact determination approach is repeatable and consistent. This will result in a confidentiality determination matrix. The table below shows a confidentiality determination matrix (DC= Data classification and NR = number of records)

Table2:Confidentiality Determination Matrix

Confidentiality Determination Matrix		
Rating	Description	Criteria
1	Very low	DC=All non-confidential
2	Low	DC=Confidential & NR= medium or low
3	Medium	DC=Confidential & NR=High
4	High	DC=Confidential with the additional classification of regulated data & NR= medium or low
5	Very high	DC=Confidential with the additional classification of regulated data & NR= High

- Data element for integrity could be the business criticality of the asset. The business criticality ranking can be gotten from the asset classification documentation. Asset classification might have a data element that indicates whether the asset is business-critical. This means that a change in the asset or system could severely impact the business function it supports. This information can also be obtained from the business impact analysis (BIA). Less mature organizations might not have an asset classification document.

- Data elements for availability. Many data elements can support the determination of the availability impact. These elements include many users using the system (more users mean a more significant impact of the loss of availability. There is also the element of business criticality. A business-critical IT asset that needs high availability will have a considerable impact on the determination of availability. The number of transactions per unit time will affect the determination of availability impact. The higher the number of transactions the system processed per unit time, the more significant the impact of availability on the system.

- These elements will lead to an Availability Determination Matrix, which contains the score, description, and criteria. A score of 5 means very high impact, which means that there is business-critical (the system is critical to the business), and the number of users is high. A score of 1 means the system is not essential to the company, and its number is low.

Determination matrices ensure that we assign scores consistently in threat and vulnerability pairs across all IT assets. Determination matrices provide guidelines that the assessment team can follow. This is what the LionsWeb assessment team did. The team could use these matrices to explain the values they assigned in the entire risk assessment.

One exciting thing that the team did was automate looking up the determination matrices and score the asset's threat and vulnerability pair. They used the Spreadsheet to automate the CIA's scoring based on the criteria spelled out in the determination matrices.

Impact Score

After determining the CIA's impact scores, we now incorporate the scores with the asset, threat, and vulnerability that affect that IT system to compute the impact score.

Computing the impact involves assigning a CIA score to each asset bases on the threat and vulnerability pair. For example, the threat of networking sniffing is more of confidentiality than availability threat. So, we assign the CIA score for each vulnerability and threat for each asset and take the highest score to be the impact score. For example, the threat is a malicious insider; the threat event is unauthorized system access, the vulnerability is possible weak password due to the absence of password complexity control. The Confidentiality score is 5, the integrity score is 0, the availability score is 0, and the impact will be 5 (which is the highest score from the CIA scores).

In general, once we have data from our data collection stage, we can extract key data elements to assign the CIA scores. We can extract the following information or data elements:

Business-critical- is the asset critical to the business(Yes or No). The answer comes from a review of the business impact assessment (BIA) and asset classification (e.g., confidential, regulated data)

The next element is the financially material and regulatory impact(is the system covered by any regulatory requirements). The number of users could be high, medium, or low. The number of users can obtain from system owners. We can get information about the number of transactions. All this information will help assign CIA scores.

Design a Control Analysis Plan

There is a general assumption on risk assessment; the assumption is that adequate controls will reduce the probability or likelihood that a threat will exploit a weakness. We have to compute the likelihood of the threat exploiting a vulnerability successfully. To calculate the likelihood, we need to know the present type and maturity of the controls. The type and maturity of the controls in place are obtained from our control survey task in the data collection phase. Controls can be grouped into access control, data protection, vulnerability monitoring, security alerts, advisories, directives, etc. Each control was given a score of either Yes or No or a rating of 1-5. The team decided to use a simple Yes or No. In terms of likelihood, more robust control will lead to a lower probability or likelihood score. That means a more robust control will reduce or weaken a threat actor's ability to exploit a vulnerability successfully. This control analysis output is a control level table that contains a score, a description, and criteria. The score could range from 1 to 5. A score of 5 means Very Strong Control, which meets the following criteria:

- the control provides robust protection against a threat
- It is highly unlikely that threat successfully exploit the vulnerability
- Control effectiveness is reviewed regularly
- The process is refined and documented
- Performance is monitored and
- Controls are consistently enforced.

Once all we rate all the controls, we match the controls with the threat/vulnerability pairs. This matching produces a control analysis table. The table has four columns: a threat source, threat event, vulnerability, controls, and controls rating. There are few things to consider when rating controls. The first consideration is that a primary control (control category) could address the threat and vulnerability pair. Once you identify the primary control, you reference the control score and add to the risk computation.

In some cases, individual controls could combine to provide primary control. Several secondary controls could supplement a weak single or primary control. An important decision is to determine if there will be a rating for the control objective's strength or rate individual controls that support the control objective.

A practical approach to doing the control analysis(identifying control, referencing the control score, and putting the risk computation score) is to automate the process. This automation can create a lookup table that matches an asset /vulnerability pair with appropriate controls and assign a control score. This control analysis task's output is a control analysis table for each system or IT asset in scope. The same columns in the control analysis table are shown below.

Table 3: Control Analysis Output

Threat source	Threat event/action	Vulnerability	Controls	Controls score

Design and compute the likelihood

The team has just completed the control score for all the identified threat and vulnerability pairs for each system. The next task is to design a scheme for the computation of the likelihood. The scheme ensures that the process is consistent and repeatable. The likelihood is that a threat actor could exploit a vulnerability and produces a threat action that can impact(affect the CIA) of a company's asset. Exposure and frequency are essential components that influence the likelihood.

Exposure is the predisposition or susceptibility of the system to the threat as a result of environmental factors. Thus, a specific environment(environment where the system operates) factors influence the system's exposure to threats. For example, an internet-facing system is more susceptible to threats because it is highly accessible to the public. The higher accessibility means greater exposure, which means a higher likelihood that the system is attacked. Other environmental factors include location and data flow, number of users, etc. The more the exposure surfaces, the higher the likelihood. Determining the exposure leads to the creation of an Exposure Determination Matrix. This matrix has a score column, a description(ranges from very likely to very unlikely), and a criteria column(description of the different ways the system is exposed). For example, a system with a score of 5 means it is very likely that the threat actor gets to it (intrusion). The criteria that led to this score is that it has been involved in some security incidents or a vulnerability has been identified in the system that can lead to intrusion. Another system with an exposure rating of 2 means that it is unlikely to be exposed to intrusion threat. The criteria it meets is that it is accessible only through the internal network.

The method used to determine the exposure can vary, but the method should be consistent throughout the systems. The team took the time to determine the system's exposure to each threat event, such as the system's exposure to intrusion, eavesdropping, interception of data, unauthorized access to a system, unchecked data modification, equipment damage, etc.

The factor that influences the likelihood is frequency. The frequency indicates how often the threat event could occur. Determining the frequency of events can be difficult. However, there are sources of information that could help with determining the frequency. Some sources include various internal security metrics (such as the number of incidents reported per unit time, number of network attacks per given time). These metrics provide an estimate of the frequency of events. Another source is the research information and trends for particular threats. There are security companies that produce this research information regularly—for example, the Verizon Annual Breach Report.

A frequency determination outcome is a frequency matrix that contains a score, description, and criteria. The score could range from 1 to 5, where a score of 5 means the very likely, while the criterion is that the threat could occur daily. A score of 1 indicates very unlikely that a threat occurs, and the criterion is that the threat could occur within five years.

After determining the frequency, we add the control score that was computed earlier. Control and likelihood are inversely related. A reasonable control reduces the likelihood of a threat actor exploiting a vulnerability to successfully produce a threat event.

The components needed to compute the likelihood are exposure, frequency, and controls. We now have all the scores for the components required to calculate the likelihood. Exposure and frequency are both proportional to likelihood. Thus, increasing exposure increases the likelihood. Likewise, increasing frequency increases the likelihood.

The formula for calculating likelihood, given frequency and exposure is

Likelihood = (Frequency + Exposure)/2.....................Equation 1

Adding control to the equation above will give

Likelihood = ((Frequency + Exposure)/2) x (Reverse Control)...............Equation2

For example, if exposure is 4, frequency 4, and controls 2

Using equation 1: Likelihood = (4+4)/2 = 8.................without controls

Using equation 2: Likelihood = ((4+4)/2) x ½ = 4 x ½ = 2............with controls

As seen from the two calculations, a system without control has a higher likelihood than with controls.

Our final table for the likelihood will have the following columns. Threat actor/source

Threat event

Vulnerability

Exposure

Frequency

Control

Likelihood

Conclusion of data analysis

We have arrived at the end of the data analysis phase of the project, and the team has done a tremendous job. They have built the threat catalog using sources such as NIST SP 800-30, they have also created their vulnerability listings through interviews, assessments, etc. They assembled threat and vulnerability pairs in a table. They considered the potential impact of threat events on confidentiality, integrity, and vulnerability. This potential impact on the CIA lied to the impact score. Finally, they computed the likelihood by assigning frequency, exposure, and control for each threat and vulnerability pair.

At this point, the team needs to calculate risk. Risk occurs when a threat source exploits a vulnerability. Risk is, therefore, the likelihood that a threat event results in an impact on the asset. Thus, to calculate risk, we need impact and likelihood.

Risk = Likelihood x Impact

The relationship between the three entities is directly proportional.

To calculate the risk, we need:

- Threat source or actor
- Threat action or event
- Vulnerability
- Impact Score
- Likelihood score
- Risk score = impact score x likelihood score.

The team has computed all the scores. They have to add them to a table with the following columns.

- Threat actor
- Threat event
- Vulnerability
- Impact score
- Likelihood score
- Risk score

The team now has to perform analysis and interpretation of the results to arrive at some meaningful conclusions. They need to do risk analysis using data to interpret, analyze, and produce conclusions.

Risk Analysis of LionsWeb

The team had to interpret the data, put together findings, and form conclusions that identified the organizational and system risks.

The team performed both system and organizational risk analysis. For system analysis, generally, we interpret data and derive findings for in-scope systems. While for organization risk analysis, we look at the overall risk to the organization. Risk scores were the leading data analysis element used. The team spun the risk scores into different views to develop additional findings of the in-scope systems.

What are the different data analysis techniques?

Risk classification

To make sense of the risk scores. We need to understand the type of data we have. This is done by putting the risk scores into High, Medium, and low groups. This classification characterizes the different levels of severity. This classification can be done using a table from ISO 27005 Annex E. The table has different areas with risk classification. If your risk score falls in an area on the table, you assign the risk classification allocated to that area. The areas are color-coded:

Black represents a risk classification of High; gray is moderate risk, and white is low risk.

The team matched their matched the risk scores for each system in-scope with the table's respective area and assigned the appropriate risk classification using this table. That led to a table with the following columns.

- Threat actor

- Threat action

- Vulnerability

- Risk score

- Risk classification

Risk Ranking

The next task is to compare the in-scope systems against each other to check the results' validity. Pay attention to any issues that deviate from expectations. Any deviations should be further verified to ensure no mistakes in the data collection or the correct information and assumptions were used in the process.

The team computed the sum of all risk scores of all threat and vulnerability pairs to get an aggregate risk score for each system. They then ranked the systems based on the aggregate risk scores. The team further reviewed the ranking to make sure there is no inaccuracies and that the data and analysis approach is accurate.

The team then studied the rankings and reviewed each system's risk.

Risk review of in-scope systems

This task focuses on reviewing the individual systems and their corresponding threats. The goal is to determine the rationale for the system's risk and make sense of the risk. Here, the assessment team wants to know how they obtain the risk score, why the system is ranked the way it is, what contributed to the system's risk rating, and what makes the system's risk significant.

The review can be done by evaluating the characteristics, controls, and system's environment of operation. Some system's environmental elements to consider are the controls in place, the system's criticality, the number of users, the confidentiality of the data, and its exposure.

This evaluation can also be done by looking for the primary contributors of impact on each system. We look at the profile survey's system profile or characteristics and identify the data classification, business-critical, number of users, and any regulations that cover the system.

Next, we examine the likelihood scores, precisely the elements contributing to the score to locate the risks. For example, how the system accessed (exposure), who uses the system(users), how the data flow through the system, and its location.

Next, examine the controls for the system using the control profile survey. We identify the controls and their strength (e.g., the system has healthy controls over data password complexity). We also identify where the system has weak or no controls (e.g., based on the system control profile, it has weak controls or documented exceptions over security awareness).

These analyses lead us to a conclusion about the system. For example, the system is a high impact system. The system is exposed to confidentiality concerns, and there is a weak password used for access to the system.

For threat and vulnerability review, the team also focused on threat and vulnerability pairs. Specifically, they identified the threat and vulnerability pairs with a high risk. The systems with such high risks could then be included in the risk treatment plan. We could also do this by getting the aggregate scores for threat and vulnerability pairs across all the systems involved. This gives a high-level view of potential problems across the entire system.

Organizational risk review

This is a review that focuses on the potential risk to the whole organization. This review is more at a strategic level than system-specific. This review generally looks at documents or any assessments that focus on organizational controls or multiple systems across the organization. Some documents can provide information that would be used to do this review. Some of the documents include security metrics, security policy exceptions, penetration tests, vulnerability assessment reports, third-party IT audit reports, etc. This review is generally unstructured. Before the review, it is essential to know the threats the organization faces. These threats and trends can be obtained from various sources such as threat catalogs, security companies, third-party vendors, etc.

Once we have a list of threats, we align them with the organization's operations. A thorough analysis of the organization's exposure against current and emerging threats demands that the assessment team has good knowledge of the organization's current business and technology plans.

Risk Prioritization and Treatment

We have come to the end of the risk analysis. We are equipped with a greater understanding of the organization's security risks (system risks and organization risks). It is now time to assemble all this information into a structured format and create risk treatment plans for the various risks. Our LionsWeb team must find ways to convey the complex risk assessment results that they just completed and accurately to the organization's stakeholders.

Risk assessment reporting (Reporting Stage) for LionsWeb Inc

At this stage of the information security risk assessment, all the results are put together into a final report. Reporting is arguably the most crucial part of the risk assessment process. With its summary memos, this report is most likely the only deliverables that the stakeholders will read. The report captures the results. The report has to be cohesive so that we can communicate our findings clearly to the stakeholders.

Outline of the Report

The report consists of an Executive summary, the methodology, the results, the risk register, conclusion, and Appendices.

The Executive summary tells the reader what is in the report, why the report was written, and the findings. The methodology describes how you derived the results, the framework used, and the activities to support the method used.

In the results section, you present the results with narratives and evidence on how the findings were derived. The risk register could be a list of findings identified during the risk assessment process. Appendices are supporting evidence for the findings.

Executive summary

The executive summary is a crucial part of the document as it is mostly the only section that is read. It has four essential components- purpose, the scope of the analysis, assessment steps, and findings summary. These components will help answer questions about what an information security risk assessment is, what the assessment is used for, what it was performed, and the results.

The purpose of the analysis is straightforward and brief, and states clearly why the risk assessment was conducted. For example:

The purpose of this analysis was to assess the risk associated with LionsWeb company remote work from home. Its resources and to protect LionsWeb's critical assets. Throughout the process, we involved stakeholders within LionsWeb. These stakeholders include but are not limited to the IT department head, Internal Audit head, IT managers, CEO, CFO, etc.

The risk assessment identified three organizational and four system-specific information security risks. The organizational risks were determined using the risk determination process. The risk determination process was done by reviewing high-level organizational risk leveraging third-party assessments, reviewing various organizational documents, analyzing current information security trends, reviewing organizational security metrics and statistics. Based on this review, LionsWeb appears to have relatively high exposure to cloud-based attacks, social engineering, data loss, malware attacks.

The system-specific risks were determined using the NIST SP800-30 to quantify risks based on likelihood, impact, and controls in place. Threat and vulnerabilities listing from ISO27005 were also used to determine risks. Based on this review, some system-specific risks determined include high exposure to the disclosure of sensitive information, remote code execution, system intrusion, and unchecked data modification that could be the CIA of infected systems and assets.

Then we summarize the analysis's scope, highlighting what the team was looking at, what was in, and what was not included in the assessment. For example, this assessment's scope included all of LionsWeb's critical assets, such as email servers, production servers, and cloud storage accounts but did not have facilities and network infrastructure. The following documents were used during the assessment: prior security risk assessment, business impact analysis(BIA), incident reports. This report represents a snapshot of the LionsWeb environment at the time of the engagement. The report does not guarantee the environment after that period.

The next component in the executive summary is the assessment steps, which describe how the assessment was conducted. For example, the following steps were followed and documented when conducting the assessment of LionsWeb's environment:

- A list of all LionsWeb's critical assets relayed to remote from home was compiled, including a brief description of the business value to LionsWeb. Each asset was assigned a risk sensitivity value.

- A series of different testing techniques were used to identify all vulnerabilities to the critical assets, including a brief description of the vulnerability and how it could affect LionsWeb.

- An impact and likelihood rating was computed for each threat and vulnerability pair. The overall risk exposure rating was determined based on each asset's confidentiality, integrity, availability, and accountability needs.

- A risk mitigation action(that will bring the risk to an acceptable level) was recommended for each identified risk.

After the scope, we discuss the assessment methodology and findings to conclude the Executive summary. We then move to the next item in the risk assessment report, the methodology.

Methodology

The methodology focuses on describing how the risk assessment was carried out. The methodology can be subdivided into the organizational and system-specific methodology.

The organizational review methodology

This methodology includes a list of activities related to organizational risk review. For example, a study of security trends was done by interviewing executive management and information security personnel, review various reports from third-party vendors.

The next activity was the review of audit findings. Various audit reports from the Internal Audit Department were reviewed. Next was the review of security incidents, including reviewing the security incidents list, interviewing the information security manager regarding security incidents. The next activity was reviewing security metrics, analyzing organizational risks, and finally, controls recommendation. This information could be structured in a table format.

System Specific review methodology

The activities that were conducted depend on the framework used. The essential thing is to identify the framework and outline the activities that were done. For example, if the framework is NIST SP800-30, then the methodology could be described as follows:

NISTSP800-30 was the standard framework that was used for this system-specific information security risk assessment. During this assessment, ISO27005 was also used as a supplementary resource.

You could provide a table of the mapping of the framework phases against the actual activities performed. For example, in the system characterization phase, activities performed included obtaining listing listings of various systems in the organization. Making final scoping decisions with the Chief Technology Officer, and the list goes on.

Results

Results provide findings with supporting evidence. These findings can be documented in a risk register. The methodology for the results is subdivided into organizational analysis and system-specific analysis.

Organizational analysis

Organizational analysis is where the observations(that serve as evidence, rationale, and proofs) that contributed to the findings are stated. For example,

The four primary activities involved in organizational risk analysis are:

Review of: Audit Findings, Security Exceptions, Security incidents, security threat and analysis, and security metrics.

It is essential to consolidate the strategic findings in this report. A table can provide a cross-reference for proposed initiatives and the corresponding risk item to mitigate. The table will have columns for risk statements, observations, and recommendations.

System-specific analysis

The structure of the write up is dependent on the framework used. For example, using NIST 800-30, the system-specific results are listed for each step(system characterization, threat identification, vulnerability identification, impact analysis, likelihood determination, controls analysis, risk determination, control recommendations) in the risk assessment process.

For example, the system characterization results analysis could be:

The team started the assessment by conducting the system characterization. This step includes performing asset scoping, interviews, asset survey of asset profile, and compiling IT asset inventories. Based on these activities, there are 17 systems in scope for the risk assessment.

You can then present the results in a table format (with a column for asset name, another column for a description of the asset, and the third column for asset owner).

For threat identification, the team described the threat agent and threat action pair. For example, the threat agent, a malicious insider, could cause a threat action of unchecked data viewing or modification. It is helpful to use a table to present the threat agent and the corresponding threat actions. Next is vulnerability identification for a specific system. Lists of current and potential vulnerabilities are introduced.

Impact analysis, Likelihood analysis, and control analysis are all intermediate that help compute the final risk determination and control recommendations. Briefly mention the results of the activities that were performed. These three analyses could have their containers (for a spreadsheet used for computations) and not necessarily be presented in the report's body.

Risk determination output

The final output of the risk determination is the risk score for all threat and vulnerability pairs for the in-scope systems. The results (e.g., a spreadsheet containing the risk calculations) could put in the Appendix.

Control Recommendations

This section provides control recommendations for the computed system-specific risks. The control recommendations could be set up as a summary. For example,

Based on the primary system-specific risks identified in the risk assessment engagement, several security controls were proposed that would lessen or remediate the risks.

The recommended controls could be presented in a table format.

Risk Register

The risk register contains the consolidation of all the findings from the risk assessment process. We present the risk and the analysis in the risk register, including the rationale for the identification, discussing current and ongoing remediation endeavors. Here is an example of how to introduce this section in the report:

Based on the risk assessment activities, the following risks were identified for the organization. Then we present the information in a table format. The table contains the risk title, score, description, risk impact, rationale, and treatment (recommended controls) for each system.

Conclusion

This section provides the assessment team's final narrative regarding risk assessment engagement. This conclusion summarizes the process and findings, some opinions, and disclaimers regarding the process

The following sections are based on the NIST SP 800-30 to integrate some parts of ISO 31000 & ISO31010. The author has made changes since these frameworks, especially NIST SP 800-30, leaves room for modification in a way that fits each organization's needs. However, the steps used in the assessment were derived from NIST 800-3

Table 4: Actions in the NIST 800-30

Task	Step				
	Preparation	Conduct		Communicate	Maintain
Identify	• Purpose of the assessment • Scope of the assessment • Assumptions and constraints • Assessment and analysis methodology/approaches • Sources of information to serve as inputs	• Threats sources • Threat events produced by sources • vulnerabilities		N/A	N/A
Determine	N/A	• The likelihood that identified threat source will cause threat events • The likelihood that threat events will be successful • The adverse impact of successful threat events on the organization's operations • Information security risk as a combination of threat event and impact		N/A	N/A
Communicate				The risk assessment results	
Share				Information learned from the assessment to support other risks activities in the organization	
Monitor					1. Risk factors determined during the risk assessment.
Update					• The components of risk assessment

Let us begin with the risk assessment process; The preparation step is the initial step in the risk assessment process. It lays the foundation for subsequent steps and actions in the risk assessment process. The essential task here is to identify the purpose of direct assessment, the scope of the assessment, the assumptions in constraints involved in the assessment, the sources of information dial serve as input to the assessment. There are five tasks in this step.

PREPARING FOR RISK ASSESSMENT

This is the initial step in the risk assessment process. It lays the foundation for subsequent actions. The essential task here is to identify the purpose of the assessment, the assessment scope, the sources of information used as input to the assessment, and the assumptions and constraints involved in the assessment.

There are five tasks in this step.

TASK 1: IDENTIFY THE PURPOSE OF THE ASSESSMENT:

Here, we want to identify the information that the assessment would produce and the decisions that the assessment will support. We know that one of the benefits of risk assessment is to support the decision-making in the organization.

What to do: state the purpose of the assessment clearly and unambiguously. Outline the goal's details to help generate the needed information or meet the intended organization objectives.

What do we need?

To identify the purpose of the risk assessment, use a defined organizational template. This template should come from the organization and contained detailed guidance on capturing and presenting the result or relevant information about the risk assessment. This template could also be used at the risk assessment communication step as part of the risk assessment report. The organization could choose another vehicle to communicate the result of the assessment. It is essential to check with the company to determine what they want the assessment team to use. If they do not have any template, then you might use any available. We will dive deeper into the risk assessment report in the subsequent step of the risk assessment process.

TASK 2 IDENTIFY THE RISK ASSESSMENT SCOPE

the main task here is to identify what will be included in the risk assessment. The scope is mostly determined by the organization that needs the assessment. The risk management strategy could also inform the scope.

Why the scope of the risk assessment?

When the scope is carefully determined, it becomes clear to both the organization and the person assessing risk to have a clear understanding of what part of the organization our system will be affected by the assessment, the tier of the organization that would be addressed. The assessment results would support these decisions.

What do you need to identify the scope?

You might do some document review. Suppose the assessment is for tier one and tier 2. In that case, you might identify the organization's governance structure search as risk a second if a particular process such as acquisition process, information security architecture.

For tier 3, you identify the information system's name in the location, the security categorization, and the information system boundary.

TASK 3 IDENTIFY SPECIFIC ASSUMPTIONS AND CONSTRAINTS

most often, organizations will have assumptions and limitations, priorities or tradeoffs, risk tolerance in the risk framing section of the risk management process.

What to do?

Cite organizational risk strategy; if there is no risk strategy, cite and document the assumptions and constraints identified by the organization. The organization's assumptions could be found in threat sources, threat events, vulnerability abilities, and predisposition conditions, potential impacts come on assessment, and analysis approaches cleared constraints identified could be in areas such as resources available for the assessment.

Where in the organization's documentation, could you find some identified constraints and assumptions that the organization has made?

According to NIST, we can find them in: the threat sources area - the type of threat sources that the organization wants to be included in the risk assessment. Check with the organization to see if they have the assumptions and constraints about threat sources in the risk management strategy document.

Threat events area

organizations have determined the types of threat events they want to be included or considered in the risk assessment. The organization might even specify how many details they like about threat events. The information on the description of threat events could range from a high-level description or general terms such as the distributed denial of service to a more in-depth description that uses tactics, techniques, and procedures in precise terms such as specific technologies. Organizations might also set particular criteria on threat events such as third events observed internally or by peer organizations.

Vulnerability area

organizations might also provide some details about the type of vulnerabilities that are to be considered in the risk assessment. If the information is available, it would be found in the risk management strategy's risk framing section. Vulnerabilities could be associated with the information system, such as hardware-software, internal controls, security procedures, etc.

What does the organization want to be included or considered in the risk assessment?

Type of vulnerabilities

The assessment team's details on the vulnerability description, any assumptions related to the vulnerability, identification process, and predisposing conditions (for example, architecture and technologies use).

Likelihood area

what do organizations want? The process used to conduct likelihood determinations and any assumptions used in the determination of likelihood

Impact area

What do organizations need? The method used to perform impact determination and any assumptions

Risk tolerance and uncertainty area:

The organization wants to know about the consideration of uncertainty, assumption of the worst case and best-case scenario.

ANALYTIC APPROACH

TASK 4 IDENTIFY INFORMATION SOURCES

information here includes a description of threats, vulnerability, and impact to be considered in risk assessment. The type of information depends on the tier in the company. For example, at tier 2, information about enterprise architecture, information security architecture, and shared services could be considered in the risk assessment. At tier 3, information about connectivity and dependency on other information.

Information about this tier can be found in system documentation, risk assessment reports, contingency plans, infrastructures, business continuity plans, architectural documentation, internal sources such as an incident report, security logs, trouble tickets, and monitoring tickets.

How can this task be performed?

This task is mostly performed through documentation reviews such as reports and logs. Interview off business and mission owners to determine if they have identified common infrastructure and support services they depend on and those they might use under specific operation circumstances.

External sources of threat information

most external sources come from cross-community organizations such as US-CERT, sector partners like defense industry base DIB, information sharing and analysis centers ISACs, research, and non-governmental organizations, such as software engineering CERT, and Security Service providers.

Vulnerability information -internal or external :

for internal, vulnerability information can be obtained from the vulnerability assessment report. For external sources are similar to threat sources.

Sources of information for predisposing conditions include describing information systems, operation environment, shared service services, shared infrastructure, and enterprise architecture.

Sources of impact information: this comes from business impact analysis BIA, information systems component inventories, and security categorization.

TASK 5: IDENTIFY THE RISK MODEL AND THE ANALYTIC METHOD

Organizations might have a defined risk model that can be used in conducting a risk assessment. An organization might also have identified a suitable model for risk assessment. Here it risk models can be converted into risk factors.

What to obtain from the organization to perform this task you can get risk models specific analytic approach including assessment method, which could be qualitative, semi-quantitative or quantitative, analysis approaches such as asset or impact-oriented, threat oriented, All vulnerability oriented. You can also obtain the assessment skill wish that can be used in the assessment of the risk. The mission of business owners alike has annotations for assessment scales with their business or mission-specific examples. Some organizations also have different assessment skills wish can be used in different situations. For instance, qualitative values for low impact information systems, semi-quantitative values (0-100) ah used for moderate hand high impact systems.

What do you have to do?

The first thing is to check for any organization-specific risk models such as tables formulas for combining risk factors. If no organizational risk model is available, specify the algorithm for combining values.

In case you need to choose a risk assessment approach or technique there, you should consider the following: Some techniques would require more data and information than orders. Some factors influence the assessment technique. These factors include the availability of data and information, the availability of resources, the need of the decision-makers.

Factors that influence risk assessment approach or technique

Decision-makers' needs are the first factor. In most cases, the decision-makers will provide some details about the decisions they intend to make with the risk assessment resort. The second factor that could influence the risk assessment approach is risk assessment objectives. Risk assessment's objectives may warrant or car for fewer details in the assessment and the type of risk that needs to be assessed or analyzed. Another factor is the number of resources and level of expertise required. The effort invested in the assessment should match the potential of risk to be analyzed. The availability of data and information is another factor. The technique chosen could need more data than order techniques. Finally, legal regulatory and contractual requirements may need specific assessment techniques.

Characteristics of the assessment approach

Irrespective of the risk assessment technique chosen, some standard features approach needs to possess. The first is that it should provide results that support a better understanding of the risk's nature and how the risk should be treated. It should be verifiable and repeatable. This implies that the assessment team should frame the technique so that others can replicate the method and obtain similar results.

RISK ASSESSMENT TECHNIQUES

Some risk assessment techniques and where there are applicable in the risk assessment process

It is important to recall that the risk assessment process comprises three key steps: risk identification, written analysis, and risk evaluation.

Risk identification - the standard techniques applied at this step include brainstorming, Checklist, Delphi, interviews structured, or semi-structured.

Risk analysis

The techniques used at this step include consequence structure what if (SWIFT), scenario analysis, BIA, root cause analysis, consequence probability matrix, cost-benefit analysis

Probability –use root cause analysis, swift, failure mode effect analysis, Cause consequences analysis, decision tree, consequence probability matrix level of risk –SWIFT, root cause analysis, failure mode effect analysis

Risk evaluation techniques

The technique used at this step includes root cause analysis, Monte Carlo simulation, Bayesian statistics, Bayes net, and risk indices.

CLASSIFICATION OF RISK ASSESSMENT TECHNIQUES

Risk assessment techniques can be classified using

 lookup method for example Checklist, scenario analysis set, for example, Root cause analysis or single loss analysis, function analysis method(for example, failure mode and effect analysis), controls assessment(for example, bow tie analysis), and the statistical method (Bayesian analysis).

Data Collection

Let us now provide more details on the data collection for our risk assessment.

Data collection activities include how to obtain resources needed to conduct a risk assessment. Data collection provides a collection of IT Asset Inventories; it can be done by conducting asset scoping workshops, interviewing stakeholders, and using asset profile surveys to collect information about the system.

The general activities are summarized in the figure.

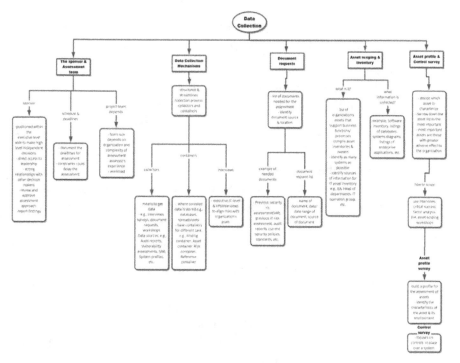

Figure 10: Overview of Data Collection

The NIST 800-30 follows the following tasks to conduct risk assessment.

- System Characterization
- Threat Identification
    - identify threat sources that are relevant to the organization.
    - Identify threat events that could threat sources could produce.
- Vulnerability Identification
    - Identify vulnerabilities within the organization that threat sources could exploit through specific threat events.
    - Identify predisposing conditions that could affect successful threat exploitation by threat sources.
- Likelihood Determination
    - Determine the likelihood that the identified threat sources would initiate specific threat events.
    - Determine the likelihood that the threat events would be successful.
- Determine the Adverse Impacts
    - Determine the adverse impacts on the organizational operations, individuals, other organizations, and even the nation from threat sources' exploitation of vulnerabilities through threat events.
- Determine information Security Risks
    - Determine information security risks by combining the likelihood of threat sources exploitation of vulnerabilities and the impact of such successful exploitation, including any uncertainties associated with the risk determination.

The risk assessment process also includes control recommendation and documentation of results.

Each step in the risk assessment process will be briefly introduced. We will discuss task(s) at each step. In each task, we will describe the action the assessor or the person performing the assessment would undertake to complete the task. We also describe what is needed (such as a document) to carry out the task. Finally, state the result or deliverable from the task.

Conducting a risk assessment is centered around two key actions. The first action is **"to identify,"** and it applies to three tasks:

- identify threat sources,
- threats events produced by the threat sources, and
- identify the vulnerabilities and predisposing conditions.

The second action, "to **determine**", which could involve computation/calculations and research applies to four tasks:

- determine the likelihood that the identified threat sources would produce threat events,
- determine the likelihood that a threat event will be successful, and
- determine the adverse impact of the organizational operations' threat events. Finally, to
- determine the information security risk as a function of the likelihood of threat event plus impact risk = likelihood of threat + impact

To conduct an assessment, we build a list of information security risks, prioritize that list by risk level to drive risk response decisions in the organization. We analyze threats, vulnerability, impact, and likelihood.

STEP 1: SYSTEM CHARACTERIZATION

System or asset characterization is usually the first task in the risk assessment. However, this task only occurs after the preparation stage of the risk assessment is completed. In the system characterization task, we begin by compiling information technology(IT) **asset inventories**. These asset inventories are compiled using methods such as:

- asset scoping workshops,

- asset profile surveys, and

- interviews.

We use the information to build a table that contains the asset name, asset description, and asset owner. A sample table is shown in table 5.

Table 5: Sample System Characterization

Asset	Asset Description	Asset Owner
Research & Development Database	This system supports the R&D initiatives for the LionsWeb company. It contains two years' worth of R7D data from the R&D department.	Dept. Head of HR

As we collect information about the asset and other organizational data which are in scope, we generate **A Data collection Matrix.** A data collection matrix is created and contains the Asset Profile Survey for each system. The Asset Profile Survey includes detailed information about each system. The asset profile should be precise and brief but captures the primary details on the system. These details will help the stakeholder to understand the process that was used, the system in scope, and a brief description of the business function that the system supports, and who is responsible for the system.

STEP 2:THREAT IDENTIFICATION

Step2 Task 1: Identify the threat source that is relevant to the organization

The next task is to identify and describe the taxonomy of threat sources or actors9such as hackers or disgruntled employees) that can initiate threat events. A detailed description of the threat source should include the intent, capability, and characteristics. But, before identifying the threat sources, it will help to know the inputs for threat source identification. These inputs could come from the organization or from external credible sources.

Potentially useful inputs for threat sources

Inputs for threat sources include

- threat sources identified in previous risk or threat assessments.

- Characteristics of threat sources annotated by the organization

- Threats related to organizational governance, core business functions, management and operational policies, procedures and structures, and external relationships.

- Open source of classified threat reports

- Threats related to business processes, support services, common security controls, enterprise architecture, and external dependencies.

- Threats related to information systems, information technologies, applications, networks, and environment where systems operate.

- Information system-specific description of adversarial and non-adversarial threat sources.

Type of threat sources

Adversarial Threat Sources

This is a type of threat source that includes individuals (outsider, insider, privileged user, trusted internal user or insider), groups (establish and ad hoc), organizations (partners, suppliers, competitors, customers), and the nation-state.

DESCRIPTION OF THE ADVERSARIAL THREAT SOURCE

the adversary threat source could be organizations, groups, individuals, or even states whose goal is to exploit the enterprise cyber resources (information and communication technologies, data, or information in the electronic form an artist resources that the company depends on). Their characteristics will include a description of their capability, assessment of the intentions, and targeting related to the threat source.

ACCIDENTAL THREAT SOURCE

This type of threat source includes privileged account users or administrators and a regular user. The threat source erroneously performs an activity that poses a risk to the organization. The characteristics of this threat source include a range of the effect of such actions.

STRUCTURAL THREAT SOURCE

These threat sources are mainly due to issues such as aging applications, equipment failure, resource depletion, or when expected operating parameters are exceeded. Examples of structural threat sources include information technology equipment (storage, communications, processing, controllers), software (operating system, general-purpose applications, networking, and specific applications), environmental controls (power supply, temperature controls). These threat sources have a different effect on enterprise resources and information.

ENVIRONMENTAL THREAT SOURCE

these include natural and human-made disasters such as fire, hurricanes, tornadoes, flooding. It also provides infrastructure failure or outage, such as electrical power outages. These sources also have a range of possible effects on enterprise resources and information.

ASSESSMENT SCALES FOR ASSESSING THE RISK FACTORS ASSOCIATED WITH THREAT SOURCES.

The relevant threat source has been identified; the assessment team can assess risk factors, including the characteristics of adversary capability, intent, and targeting. Non-adversarial characteristics are also evaluated using an assessment scale.

Table 6:Assessment scale used to assess adversarial and non-adversarial risk factors

ID	Qualitative value	Semi-quantitative value	Quantitative value
	Very high	96-100	10
	High	80-95	8
	Medium	21-79	5
	Low	5-20	2
	Very low	0-4	0

Assessing Adversary Capability

Assessing the characteristics of the adversary capability involves having an assessment scale. The scale could use qualitative or quantitative or semi-quantitative values. The qualitative values range from very high to very low. The very high values correspond to a semi-quantitative value of 96 to 100 and a quantitative value of 10. This qualitative value of very high indicates that the adversary possesses a highly sophisticated level of expertise, sufficient resources, and can execute well-coordinated, persistent, and successful attacks. On the other hand, a qualitative value of very low, which corresponds to a semi-quantitative value of zero to four, any quantitative value of 0, means that the adversary has very little expertise, limited resources, and opportunities to carry out, and six sustain a successful attack.

Assess the characteristics of adversary intent.

We also use an assessment scale for adversary intent characteristics. The assessment scare users qualitative or semi-quantitative or quantitative values. For example, a qualitative value of very high, which is equivalent to assume a qualitative, quantitative value of 9061 hundred or quantitative value of 10, means that the adversary intention is to severely impede, undermine, or damage a critical business program or enterprise.

The adversaries want to maintain their presence in the enterprise information systems and exploit it as much as possible. It aims to disclose vital information to the best of its ability and does not want to be detected.

On the other hand, another series intent qualitative value of very low or a semi-quantitative value of zero to four or quantitative value of 0 means that the adversary intends to disrupt, ruin or usurp a cyber enterprise resource but is not concerned about being detected or having their tactics techniques and procedures disclosed or exposed.

Assessing the characteristics of adversarial targeting

In an adversary targeting, the adversary analysis information about their target using different means. The adversary could use information obtained through reconnaissance to target a specific organization, program, business function, ETC. Depending on the adversary's competence or capability, they may not even target any particular organization. The assessment team focuses on placing a qualitative, semi-quantitative, or quantitative value on the adversaries targeting. For example, a qualitative value of very high means the adversaries use reconnaissance and attacks to obtain information about their target, analyze that information, and persistently target a specific enterprise, program, employee, business function, or organization partners.

Non-adversarial threat source

We have talked about adverse erythroid sources so far. Now let us talk about non-adversarial threat sources that could be considered during a risk assessment. For these non-adversarial threat sources, the assessment team will assess the range of effects and assign an assessment value using the assessment scale previously discussed. Some non-adversarial threat sources include errors made by employees or organizations partners or other stakeholders and accidents.

Qualitative or semi-quantitative or quantitative values will be assigned to these sources. For example, a qualitative value of very high means that the error's effect is far-reaching or sweeping. The impact of the error involved almost all the enterprise cyber resources at all three tiers. For a qualitative value of very low, means the effect of the error involved only a few enterprise cyber resources, and no critical resources are affected.

Table 7: Summary the adversarial threat source identification

Identification of Adversarial threat Sources					
ID	Source of information for Threat source/actor	In scope	Capability	Intent	Targeting
	e.g adversarial identified in previous risk/threat assessment	Yes/no	Very high	moderate	high

Step 2 Task 2:Identify potential threat events, relate them to the organization and corresponding threat sources that can initiate these threats events

An event can include one or more occurrences and have many causes.

Threat events are generally characterized by threat sources that Launch event. Adversarial threat events are marked by the tactic techniques and procedures used to execute attacks. In risk assessment, these threat events are vividly and precisely described. Threat events can be mapped onto the various tiers in the organization.

At Tier 1, threat events are those that can affect the entire organization. It includes threat events that traverse information systems, exploit the interconnection among systems, and influence business functions. At tier 3, threat events are those that affect specific information systems or operating environments. The relationship between threat sources and threat events could be I want too many where one threat source performs many threats events, are many to many where many threat sources initiate many threats events.

Identification of threat events inputs

These are inputs that can be used to identify threat events. This input can be recognized at the various tiers of the organization. For example, at the organizational level or Tier 1, we can identify threats events from credible information from threat sources such as classified threat reports, previous threat or risk assessment performed in the organization, annotated adversary threat events conducted by the organization, threat events from previous enterprise risk assessments.

From Tier 2 search events information specific to business processes, support services, standard controls, and other Tier 2 services and infrastructure. From tier 3 inputs for threat, event identification can be threat event information specific to threats link to information systems, information system components, and another tier three resources. Input for potential threat events can also come from incident reports. The table below shows some common threat event characterized by the tactics, techniques, and procedures(TTPs)

Thus, inputs for threat event identification include but not limited to the following

- Open source threat reports
- Previous threat/risk assessments

- Threats related to organizational governance, core business functions, management and operational policies, procedures and structures, and external relationships.

- Exemplary adversarial and non-adversarial threat events annotated by the organization.

- Threat events related to business processes, common infrastructure, enterprise architecture, support services, external dependencies, and common controls.

- Business process-specific description or characterization of adversarial and non-adversarial threat events(such those threat events that have been seen by the organization, seen by the organization peers, reported by trusted sources, or predicted by trusted sources).

- Threats related to information systems, information technologies, applications, networks, and environment of operation.

Stages of adversary threat events.

Threat events characterized by the tactics, techniques, and procedures can be divided into different stages for simplicity and easy understanding. these stages include

STAGE 1: THE ADVERSARY PERFORMS RECONNAISSANCE AND GATHERS INFORMATION ABOUT THE TARGET

At this stage, some threats event includes sniffing exposed networks using network sniffing tools to access exposed data channels to identify components, protections, and resources. At this stage, the adversary can also scan the perimeter network using open source or commercial tools. The scanning goal is to better understand the organization's information technology infrastructure and carry out successful attacks. The adversary can also gather information about their target by using publicly available information about a target. This information gathering would lead the adversary to the next stage, which is crafting attacks.

STAGE 2 CRAFTING ATTACK TOOLS

at this stage, the adversary has much information about their target. The adversary then proceeds to create spear phishing, phishing attacks against a high-value target such as senior management, and fake communications from legitimate sources to obtain valuable information such as personally identifiable information and other credentials. These attacks mostly happen via email attachment, directing users to fake sites to steal their credentials.

STAGE 3 DELIVER MALICIOUS CAPABILITIES

the goal here is for the adversary to provide or install malware on the target system using different means. The adversary uses email, web traffic, FTP, or removal media to deliver them our way the adversary wants to get into the target's system.

STAGE 4 EXPLOIT AND COMPROMISE.

Here, the adversary continues to find ways to access the target system and explore different possibilities to accomplish this goal.

STAGE 5 CONDUCT AN ATTACK

at this stage, the adversaries coordinate and direct attacks or activities on the target system. The threat events here include intercepting communication when they are unencrypted or are using weak encryption. This interception can be done on authorized ports, services, or protocols to carry out attacks on the target, perform distributed denial of service attacks using compromised information systems, conduct physical attacks on target facilities, conduct brute force attacks, etc.

STAGE 6 - ADVERSARY ACCOMPLISHES THE MISSION, OBTAINS ORGANIZATIONAL INFORMATION, CAUSES AN ADVERSE IMPACT.

At this stage, the adversary achieved its goal. Depending on the intent of the attack threat event, there could be several goals. Some of the threat events include obtaining organization sensitive information through sniffing or exfiltration, causing integrity loss by making unauthorized changes to data, getting unauthorized access to organization systems and resources, and so on.

STAGE 7 -MAINTAIN A PRESENCE IN THE ORGANIZATION SYSTEM.

The adversary finds ways to maintain their presence or their capabilities in the organization systems. Threat events at this stage include obfuscating adversary activities and actions to prevent any detection of their intrusion by any intrusion detection system or any auditing capabilities that the organization has put in place. Adversaries also find ways to adapt your behavior to any security measures.

STAGE 8 COORDINATE AND EXPAND THE CAMPAIGN.

The adversary at this stage is expanding the attack to other organization systems. Some threat events here include shifting or moving malicious command sources from compromised systems to other systems. The adversary also extends attack campaigns across multiple organizations to gain more information about their target. The adversary continuously changes their attacks in response to any organization's security measures and using more coordinated attacks impede the organization's operations.

Non-adversarial threat events

Threat events here range from an authorized user erroneously spilling sensitive information to a tornado occurring at a primary facility causing the operations to stop.

The relevance of threat event.

At this point, the assessment team or individual performing the risk assessment has identified the threat event. Now is the time to assess the relevance of the threat events to the organization. This assessment of relevance is done by assigning a value to the threat event. The values that are mostly assigned are confirmed a value that indicates the daddy organization has seen the threat event before or the tactics techniques and procedures.

Expected which is a value that indicates that the organization peers or partners have seen the threat events anticipated suggests that a trusted source has reported a threat event

predicted indicates that a trusted source has predicted a threat event possible means that a somewhat credible source has described the threat event NA in the case that the threat event is not applicable

Table 8: Summary of Threat Event Identification.

ID	Source of information Threat event	Threat source	Relevance
Defined by organization	e,g. Identified in previous threat assessment. Perform network sniffing of exposed networks	Adversarial	Confirmed

STEP 2: IDENTIFY VULNERABILITIES AND PREDISPOSING CONDITIONS.

The tasks in this step focus on identifying the vulnerabilities and predisposing conditions that affect the likelihood of identifying threat events resulting in an adverse impact on the organization. The assessment team will conduct a vulnerability assessment to understand the extent to which organization business processes, information systems, and assets vulnerable today already identified threat sources and threat events.

Exploited vulnerability impact can be mapped to the various tiers in the organization. For example, exploit availability impact at tier 1 can span the entire organization and could be far-reaching. At Tier 2, these exploited vulnerability impacts will cross information system boundaries. At tier 3, the impact of the of exploited vulnerabilities could be on information technologies that the organization uses in its information systems, the systems operation environment or environment where the systems operate, the nature of the system-specific security controls, which include a lack of control or weakness in the control. Exploited vulnerabilities in tier three could result in the compromise of a specific system.

Vulnerabilities are extensive and complicated, especially if there is a continuous increase in organization size, and the organization also has complex business operations and information systems supporting the systems. Therefore, vulnerability is a function of the organization's size, business operations complexity, and the information system supporting the business processes.

The organization's complexity and size imply that the number of vulnerabilities can be vast and overwhelming to assess or analyze. The organization can resolve this complexity of vulnerability analysis in several ways. The first option is for the organization to understand the general nature of the vulnerability. The general nature of the vulnerability here would be the vulnerability scope, number, and type relevant to the risk assessment. The organization can also perform a catalog of relevant vulnerabilities. Then the organization Maps the vulnerabilities to relevant threat events to reduce potential risk to be assessed. predisposing conditions within an organization can also affect the likelihood that one or more threat event initiated by three sources impact the organization

This task is to describe some useful input that can be used to identify vulnerabilities and predisposing conditions. The input can be from the three tiers or organizational level, business process level, or information system level, which correspond to Tier 1, Tier 2, and tier 3. At the corporate level or Tier 1, vulnerability identification inputs can be from credible sources of vulnerability information such as open-source vulnerability, previous vulnerability or risk assessment, and business impact assessment, business impact analysis (BIA).

From the business or mission process level or Tier 2, vulnerability information sources could be the vulnerability information and guidance specific to business processes such as vulnerability related to organization business processes, shared infrastructure, support services, external dependencies, etc. Information about the vulnerability can also come from the business continuity plan, BCP four individual processes, or business units.

At the information system level or tier 3, the vulnerability information can be obtained from vulnerabilities related to information systems, specific information technologies, applications, the environment of operations, and networks. Vulnerability information can also be obtained from the security assessment report, including any deficiencies in access controls identified as vulnerability. Other sources of information for vulnerability include the result of monitoring activities, incident reports, contingency plans, red team reports, vendor or manufacturer reports, disaster recovery plans, order reports from the analysis of information systems, and so on.

In summary, inputs for vulnerabilities and predisposing conditions include but not limited to the following:

- Open source vulnerabilities.
- Previous risk/vulnerability assessments, Business impact analysis(BIA).
- Vulnerabilities related to organizational governance, core business functions, procedures, external business relationships.

- Business continuity plan (BCP).
- Vulnerabilities related to organizational business processes, enterprise architecture segments, support services, external dependencies, and common controls.
- Vulnerabilities related to information systems, information technologies, applications, networks, and environment of operation.

Step2 Task 2: Assess the severity of identified vulnerabilities-assessment scale

Here an assessment scale is used to assess the severity of identified vulnerabilities. In the assessment, they use qualitative, semi-quantitative, and quantitative values. There is also a description of the values assigned. The description focuses on vulnerability level, whether the vulnerability is exposed, exploitable, and the impact of its exploitation. The narrative also zooms in on whether relevant security control or other remediation measures are implemented, plant, or any security measures can be identified to remediate the vulnerability. The scale can be found in table F-2 of the NIST 800-30.

Table 9: Assessment scale for Identified Vulnerabilities

Qualitative	Semi Quantitative	Quantitative
Very High	96-100	10
High	80-95	8
Medium	21-79	5
Low	5-20	2
Very Low	0-4	0

SUMMARY OF VULNERABILITY IDENTIFICATION

This is when the assessment team summarizes or documents the vulnerability identified and the assessment of the vulnerabilities. The results could be summarized in a table like the one shown below

Table 10: Summary of Identified Vulnerabilities

Identifier	Vulnerability	Vulnerability Source of information	Vulnerability severity
e.g. VN001	Weak password	Previous vulnerability assessment	High

Step2 Task3: Identify and characterize predisposing conditions.

What taxonomy can the assessment team identify and characterize the predisposing conditions? The taxonomy highlights the type of predisposing conditions and their characteristics. We could generally classify the predisposing conditions into three types: technical, information-related, operational, or environmental.

Information related to predisposing conditions

this involved the need to handle information in a specific way due to sensitivity regulatory or legal requirements and other organizational or contractual agreements. Information here includes personally identifiable information, proprietary information, classified information, etc.

Technical predisposing conditions involve the need to use technologies in specific ways—for example, compliance with specific technical standards and particular security functionality to come on controls. Functional predisposing conditions such as single-user or multi-user standalone or restricted functionality also examples of predisposing technical conditions.

Operational or environmental predisposing conditions

This involves the ability to rely on procedural, physical, and personal controls that the operational environment provides. For example, physical control could be to use a mobile site or a static site. Besides, an operational control could be that there should be vetting of population or making sure that they have clearance.

Assess the pervasiveness of predisposing conditions

After identifying and classifying the predisposing conditions, it is essential to assess the pervasiveness or apply the organizational tear's predisposing conditions. The assessment team can use an assessment scale with qualitative semi-quantitative or quantitative values to do the assessment. Assessment scales include values and a brief description.

Summary of step 2: Identifying vulnerabilities and predisposing conditions.

The first thing we do here is to identify vulnerabilities and predisposing input using sources from various organization tiers. Vulnerabilities can be identified using organizationally defined information sources, or the assessment team can create a vulnerability identification by exploring a vulnerability source of information.

Next, we assess the severity of the identified phone abilities using an assessment scale or a tailored assessment scale by the organization. Then we identify predisposing conditions using a taxonomy of predisposing conditions, which include the type of predisposing condition and a brief description. This taxonomy serves as the source of information for predisposing condition identification. Then we assess their pervasiveness of the predisposing conditions. Pervasiveness tells us where in the organization tier the predisposing conditions apply. We can then update column 8 in table I-5 for adversarial risk or column 6 in table I-7 for non-adversarial risk.

STEP 3: DETERMINE THE LIKELIHOOD

A likelihood score offer threat involves combining the likelihood that the event will happen because something or someone initiated the event and the likelihood that the event's initiation or triggered event would adversely impact the organization, individuals, other organizations, or even the nation.

So, overall likelihood = likelihood that event occurs + livelihood that event results in adverse impacts.

The assessment of the overall likelihood of threat event is done using potentially useful input to the livelihood. Use an assessment scale to determine the likelihood of threat events occurring due to adverse or non-adversarial threat sources, the likelihood of the threat event resulting in adverse impact.

The determination of likelihood values (very high, high, medium, low, and very low) depends on the organization's attitude towards risk. This attitude towards risk includes the organization's risk tolerance and uncertainty tolerance. The organization also has specific thick tolerance towards the various risk factors. Organizations have different rules for weighting risk factors. For example, an organization might put more weight on the value for the likelihood that a threat event occurs or assume that there will be adverse impacts if a threat event occurs very high or high. Some organizations only considered the likelihood of impact. Other organizations can make a match how they want to consider the likelihood values.

Step 3 task 1: Determine the likelihood that threat events result in adverse impacts on the organization.

To determine the likelihood that threat events will adversely impact the organization, the assessment team can use the threat sources' characteristics (capability, intent, and target) to cause a threat event. The team can also use the identified vulnerabilities and predisposing conditions and the controls or countermeasures that the organization has implemented or planned to implement to prevent the threat events. So, the likelihood of threat events causing an impact depends on the adversary's characteristics, vulnerabilities, and controls.

"Likelihood of threat event impacting organization = a function of threats source characteristics, vulnerabilities, controls."

Overall likelihood determination.

From my experience, the likelihood of an adversary initiating a threat event or threat event occurring due to the non-adversarial source is higher than the likelihood of the triggered event resulting in an adverse impact on the organization. However, during the assessment, the company's attitude towards risk tolerance is what matters.

Now let us discuss the various tasks involved in determining the likelihood of threat events occurring and resulting in adverse impact.

Identify input for livelihood determination

the first task in the overall likelihood determination is to identify and describe the potential useful input to the likelihood determination. These inputs can come from various organizational tiers (organization no level, mission or business process level, and information system level).

From the organizational level, the input for likelihood determination will include Tier 1 livelihood information guidance such as management or operational policies, assessment scale for assessing the likelihood of threat initiation and occurrence, assessment scale for assessing their overall likelihood occurring or being initiated. This is not an exhaustive list; check with the accompany for any other imports.

From Tier 2, the business process level, inputs for likelihood determination can be specific Tier 2 likelihood information and guidance such as any likelihood information associated with business processes, support services, common controls, etc.

From the information system level or tier 3, the input could be historical data on successful and unsuccessful cyberattacks(attack detection rates), vulnerability assessment, security assessment reports (vulnerability due to deficiencies in assess controls), incident reports, and network applications, etc.

The assessment team can request and review these various inputs and then determine the likelihood of threat event initiation by an adversary using an assessment scale to assign a score, which can be qualitative, semi-quantitative, or quantitative.

Assessment scale for determining the likelihood of adversary initiating threat event.

Threat events initiation can be assessed using an assessment scare with qualitative, semi-quantitative, or quantitative values. The qualitative values range from very high (corresponding to a semi-quantitative value of 96 -100, or a quantitative value of 10) two very low (corresponding to a semi-quantitative a quantitative value of 80-95 and 8).

Qualitative value of very high means that the adversary is almost certain to initiate the threat event. For example, a hacker is nearly sure to start a phishing attack (threat event)on a company. A qualitative value of very low indicates that the adversary is highly unlikely to initiate the threat event.

Determine the likelihood of the threat event occurring due to a non-adversary source

The next task is to use an assessment scale to determine the likelihood of the threat event occurring due to a non-adversary source (arrow, accident, an act of nature). a similar assessment scale for adversary's sources is used. The assessment scale has qualitative, semi-quantitative, and quantitative values that the assessment team in consultation with the company can choose to use. Qualitative values go from very high to very low. Very high values indicate that the error, accident, or natural act is almost certain to occur more than 100 times a year. A high value means that the error or mistake, accident, or act of nature is highly likely to occur between 10 to 100 times per year.

Assessment scale for assessing the likelihood of a threat event resulting in an adverse impact on the organization.

The assessment scale indicates if the threat event that is initiated or as a card will almost certainly, highly likely, unlikely, or highly unlikely have adverse impacts. The scale could use qualitative, quantitative, or semi-quantitative values.

Assessment scale for assessing the overall likelihood of threat event occurring and resulting in adverse impacts on the organization

This assessment scale combines the likelihood of threat of initiation or occurrence with the threat events resulting in adverse impact.

STEP 4:DETERMINE THE ADVERSE IMPACT OF THREAT EVENTS

We have identified the threat sources and vulnerabilities that the threat sources can exploit to generate threat events. We have identified the likelihood of threat events being initiated by an adversary or occurring due to a non-adversary source. We determined the likelihood that the threat events that have been undertaken will adversely impact the organization.

It is now time to determine the adverse impact of the threat event. Adverse impact is described in terms of the potential harm to the organization's assets, operations, other organizations, or individuals. To determine the adverse impacts, we need to consider three variables; the threat Source's characteristics (Competency, intent, and targeting), identified vulnerabilities and predisposing conditions, and the controls or countermeasures put in place 2 impede threat events. We consider the severity of the impact, which is influenced by where the event occurs and whether the event's effect can be spread or contained.

The severity of impact = a function of where the threat event occurs + weather effect are contained or Spread.

To assess the impact, we identify the asset, information data, shared applications, or potential targets of three sources that could include information resources such as data and applications come on people that could be affected. We then identify three sources, vulnerability, predisposing conditions, threat events, and the likelihood of occurrence.

Valuable input that can be used to determine impacts.

Useful input that can be used for impact determination can come from the three tiers of the organization. Inputs from Tier 1 includes critical business functions that have been identified, guidance on enterprise-wide levels of impact, impact guidance information specific to Tier 1(such as impact information to core business functions, operational policies, procedures, and structures). Other inputs include some examples of the adverse impact that the organization has identified and annotated.

Input from Tier 2, we can also impact after it relates to Tier 2 from identifying high-value asset document or impact information specific to Tier 2 resources. Tier 2 resources include enterprise architecture segment, support services, business processes, shared services, etc.

Input information about the impact to tier three could come from historical data on successful and unsuccessful attacks, security assessment reports, Continuous monitoring activity reports, automated and automated data feed, Warner ability assessment reports, disaster recovery plans, etc.

EXAMPLES OF THREAT EVENTS ADVERSE IMPACT TO THE ORGANIZATION

Several threat events impact or harm the organization, individuals, other organizations, or even the nation. Some men tabs of impact include harm two assets (damage to or loss of information systems or networks, information technology or equipment, information assets, intellectual property, physical facilities). Harm to mission or business operations can impede the ability to perform business functions in a sufficiently only man, with sufficient confidence or correctness, and within plan resource constraints. Home to operations could also limit the ability to perform business functions in the future, such as restoring business functions, inability to complete future tasks in a sufficiently timely manner, with sufficient confidence, and within planned resource constraints. Then there is harm to other organizations. There could be the harm in the form of financial cost or loss, non-compliance with applicable laws or regulations, and contractual requirements. Another harm to operations includes damage to trust relationships and reputation.

Assessment scale for the impact of threat events.

At this point, we have covered much ground in terms of getting the necessary component needed to assess the impact of the threat events. We now use an assessment scale discord the impact of the threat effects. As usual, the assessment scale can use qualitative, semi-quantitative, or quantitative values. The qualitative values range from very high to very low. A high value indicates that the threat event could be expected to have multiple severe adverse effects on the organization's assets, operations, individuals, other organizations, or even the nation. A qualitative value of very low indicates that the threat event could be expected to have a negligible adverse effect on organizational assets, operations, individuals, other organizations, or even the nation.

STEP5: DETERMINE THE RISK TO THE ORGANIZATION FROM THREAT EVENTS

The degree by which a potential threat event threatens an organization depends on the level of risk associated with the identified threat events. Risk determination has uncertainties which, for the most part, are expressed by the organization. These uncertainties could include subjective judgments and organizational assumptions. When a list of threat events is presented to the organization, they decide what to do based on its mission. The organization can prioritize the risk based on the risk or value. For example, the organization might focus on high-value risk ricks from the threat event = likelihood of the event occurring + impact resulting from the event.

Each risk corresponds to a particular threat event and associated level of impact if the threat event occurs. Most often, the risk level is less than the impact level. However, if multiple moderate-level risks occur, the resulting impact could be higher to the organization. Therefore, it is crucial to consider a threat even as considerable damage and an impact level consider the cumulative degree of harm.

In identifying threat sources, adversary characteristics (capability, intent, targeting), the organization should highlight essential information related to risk assessment uncertainties. The uncertainties could come from subjective determinations, missing information, assumptions. It might be helpful to have a documented assumption made during the assessment.

Now let us look at the import that can help us determine risk.

Useful input for risks and uncertainties determination

Potentially useful inputs used to determine risk can come from the three tiers in the organization. Inputs from the organization level or Tier 1 includes guidance on enterprise-wide levels of risk and uncertainties. Other inputs from this tier are the organization annotated assessment scale for assessing the level of risk, identified sources of risk and uncertainty information such as precise information that could be used to determine the likelihood of adversary intent and targeting objectives.

Inputs from the business process level or tier two could include risk-related guidance specific to tier two resources, such as risk related to business processes, shared infrastructure, controls, and support services.

Finally, input from the information system level or Tier 1 could include risks related guidance specific to the information system level. For example, risk-related guidance information to information technologies, information system components, applications, the environment of operations, and networks.

Assessment scale used to assess the likelihood and impact of risk (levels of risk).

The assessment scale can use qualitative, quantitative, or quantitative values to assess its risk levels. The first part of the assessment is to rate the likelihood that a threat event will adversely impact the organization.

This rating could range from very high to very low. Next, read the level of impact from very high to very low

Assessing the risk level involves qualitative or semi-quantitative or quantitative values that indicate whether a threat event could be expected to have multiple severe or catastrophic adverse effects on organizational operations an asset. A high-risk level means that the threat event could be expected to have a severe adverse impact on organizational assets and operations. A moderate risk level means that the threat event could have serious adverse effects on corporate assets and operations. A low-risk level indicates that the threat event could have a limited adverse effect on the organizational assets and operations. A very low-risk level suggests that the threat event could be expected to have a negligible adverse impact on corporate assets and operations.

Adversarial Risk Input Elements.

This is when we summarize the adversarial risk in a table, for instance. Then we decide to use a table to summarize the adversarial or malicious risk. The table will contain threat events, threat source, threat source characteristics, and threat event relevance as per organization criteria (irrelevance of threat event meets organization criteria).

Then we add the likelihood of attack initiation, vulnerability, and predisposing conditions. We include the severity and pervasiveness (severity of vulnerability and pervasiveness of predisposing conditions). Then add the likelihood that initiated attacks succeed (that threat event once started will adversely impact). We further include the overall likelihood (a combination of the likelihood of attack initiation and likelihood of initiated attacks succeeding). We add the impact level (potential harm to organization operations, assets, individuals, other organizations). Finally, we add risk (level of risk as a combination of likelihood and impact).

Non-Adversarial Risk Essential Data Elements or Input

Similar to the adversary's element input table, the non-adversarial risk data element table summarizes the vital data element components used for non-adversarial risk determination from the threat event. There is a total of 11 elements that contribute to the non-adversarial report. These elements include:

- the identified threat events
- identified threat sources that could trigger threat events and
- identified the range of threat source effects.

The next features include determining relevance that meets the organization's criteria, the determined likelihood that threat events will occur, identified vulnerabilities, and predisposing conditions that threat sources could exploit. Then, there is the assessed severity of vulnerabilities and pervasiveness of predisposing condition. The other element component includes the determined likelihood that the threat event leads to adverse impact. The overall likelihood shows that the threat event, once triggered, results in adverse effects (likelihood of threat event occurring plus the likelihood of threat event resulting in adverse impact). The last two components or element components are the determined level of impact, which indicates the potential harm to organizational assets, operations, people, other organizations from the threat event. Finally, the determined level of risk, which is a combination of likelihood and impact.

STEP 6: RISK ASSESSMENT REPORTS: COMMUNICATE AND SHARE RISK ASSESSMENT RESULTS.

So far, we have gone from identifying threat source, threat event, the likelihood of threat event occurring, the likelihood of event resulting in potential harm to the determination of the level of risk. We are now in the third step, which is to communicate and share the risk assessment result. The objective of communicating risk assessment results is to provide the appropriate risk-related information to inform the organization's risk-based decisions. There are two main tasks to be performed in this step. The first task is to prepare and communicate the risk assessment result. The second task is to share the information produced in the risk assessment course to support risk-related activities in the company or organization.

Step 6 Task 1: Communicates the risk assessment result to support risk response from decision-makers in the organization.

There are numerous ways to communicate risk assessment results. Some methods include risk assessment reports and executive briefings in the dashboard. Often organizations would guide the requirement for risk reporting. If available, this guidance can be found in risk framing, specifically in the risk management strategy.

The type of information included in a risk assessment reports

Risk assessment report (or any other means of communicating the results) has essential elements described in three main sections. The three sections are the executive summary, the main body of the report, and supporting documentation. Sections of the risk assessment report

SECTION : EXECUTIVE SUMMARY

There are six subsections in the executive summary.

The first subsection is to list the date of the risk assessment. This next section summarizes the purpose of the risk assessment. Then there is a description of the scope of the risk assessment. The scope can be broken down into three tiers of the organization. Here, we identify the scope at each tier or level of the organization. For instance, at tier three, we can identify the information system name and location, security categorization, and information system boundary for tier three risk assessment.

The scope for tier three assessment involves the IT identification of the organizational processes or governance structures associated with their assessment. Structures and processes could be enterprise architecture, information security architecture, acquisition process, business process, business functions, systems engineering process.

The next section indicates whether the assessment is a follow-up to the previous assessment (subsequent assessment) or an original or initial assessment. If the assessment is a follow-up, then highlight the conditions that led to the update and add a reference to the previous risk assessment report.

The next section in the executive summary is a description of the overall level of risk. For example, the overall risk level is very high, high, moderate, low, very low here, and finally identifies or lists the number of risks identified for each risk level. For example, how many risks were rated as low, very low, moderately high, or very high?

Body of the report

The second section of the risk assessment report is the content of the body of the report. This section begins with a brief description of the assessment's purpose, the questions that the assessment had to answer. Questions to address here include how the particular information technology used in a specific function or process would affect organizations' business functions or operations. Also, how to use the result of the risk assessment in the risk management framework. In other words, how can the result be used to customize security controls baselines and serve as a foundation for subsequent risk assessment for an organizational function, process, etc.?

The next item in the report's body is to identify any assumptions and constraints used in the assessment. The assumptions help the decision-makers to make well-informed decisions. The risk assessment informs their risk response. There is also a description of the risk tolerance input, highlighting the range of consequences to be taken into consideration in the risk assessment. Also, their body includes a brief description of the risk analytic approach and risk model. The revelation of the assumptions and constraints can be either done by providing a reference or an appendix, the value scales, identifying risk factors, and how the team combined them.

Furthermore, for any risk related decision made during the assessment process, provide a reason for the decision. The next item describes any business functions or processes considered in their assessment, with their related dependencies and technologies that support these functions and processes. Likewise, for any organization's information systems, describe the system, including the function of the system support, the flow of information through these systems, any dependencies, commercial services, or common infrastructure.

Also, provide a summary of the risk assessment result. This summary can be done using tables or graphs. The main thing is to use a convenient form that will lead to an easy understanding of the decision-makers' risk assessment results. It is essential that the graph or table highlights, for example, the number of threat events at different risk levels and several threat events for a different combination of likelihood and impact.

Finally, identify the reasonable time frame for the risk assessment. This indicates the timeframe for which the result of the assessment can support decisions made. Also, identify the risks due to adversarial and non-adversarial threats.

Support documentation or appendix

This is the last section of the risk assessment report. This is where you provide a list of references and sources of information. Also listed members of the team who conducted the risk assessment. Some examples of supporting evidence in his assessment details include

table identification of adversary threat sources, a table showing the identification of non-adversarial three sources, a table showing the identification of threat events, a table showing the identification of vulnerabilities, a table showing the identification of predisposing conditions, and a table showing the identification or adverse impact.

Step 6 task 2: Share Risk-related Information Generated During Assessment

The principal objective is to share the risk-related information from the risk assessment with the organizational personnel in this task. The information-sharing uses reports and briefings and could also involve adding evidence to the existing risks related to data repositories. When sharing information, it is essential to provide supporting documentation of information sources, analytic approach, and processes. Also, provide intermediate results such as threat sources, threat events, vulnerability, predisposing conditions, the likelihood of threat events being initiated, the impact of threat events on the organization. Providing supportive documentation helps maintain risk. Risk related information sharing can be done within the organization or with other organizations.

STEP 7:MAINTAIN THE RISK ASSESSMENT.

This step's primary goal in the risk assessment process is to keep the organization's risk knowledge current and up to date. In the organization but no review, risk management decisions are made on an ongoing basis. Risk assessment resources provide vital information about the risk that supports the continuing evaluation of risk management decisions.

Another essential task in the risk management process is risk monitoring. Risk monitoring contributes to risk management by providing information that helps determine the effectiveness of organizational risk responses. Risk monitoring, which is done continuously, identifies changes that impact risk. The difference could be to the organizational information systems and their operating environment. To maintain risk assessment in the organization, risk factors must be monitored regularly, and any changes to these factors are identified and understood. The monitoring activities should be used to update risk assessment components.

Step 7 Task 1: Monitor Risk Factors that Affect Risk in the Organization

This task's objective is to conduct ongoing monitoring of the risk factors (vulnerabilities, threat sources, trade events) that affect the risk to organizational operations, assets, individuals, and other organizations. The essential contribution of ongoing risk monitoring is to have reliable incredible risk-based information that can be used to make risk-based decisions. Monitoring risk factors could also provide critical information on how various conditions change and how change could affect the organization's essential functions and processes and impede its ability to conduct business. Monitoring could also produce valuable information that can update and refresh the risks assessment and capture changes in risk measures effectiveness.

Step 7 Task 2: Update Existing Risk Assessment.

This task's objective is to use the results of the monitoring of risk factors to update the existing risk assessment. The risk assessment is updated regularly. The organization determines when the updates are done. The organization also determines the frequency and circumstances under which risk assessments are updated. This decision is influenced by factors such as the importance of core business functions, level of risk, policies, directions, or guidance. Pieces of advice could outline the conditions that can trigger the need for a risk assessment update. The risk assessment task, such as the scope purpose constraints assumptions, can be revisited at a defined time interval to determine whether these tasks need to be reassessed.

Conclusively, to maintain risk assessment, the organization has to identify significant risk factors that have been identified for continuous monitoring. The transition also has to recognize the circumstances under which the risk assessment would be updated and the frequency of risk factor monitoring. This updated risk assessment and risk factor monitoring would help the organization reconfirm the risk assessment assumption's scope and purpose. The organization has to ensure that risk assessment is performed appropriately, and the results communicated to specified organizational personnel.

INDEX

www.ingramcontent.com/pod-product-compliance
Lightning Source LLC
Chambersburg PA
CBHW071002050326
40689CB00014B/3461